ACHIEV_____

FOR ALL

ACHIEVEMENT FOR ALL

Raising Aspirations, Access and Achievement

Sonia Blandford and Catherine Knowles

BLOOMSBURY
LONDON • NEW DELHI • NEW YORK • SYDNEY

Published 2013 by Bloomsbury Education
Bloomsbury Publishing plc
50 Bedford Square, London WC1B 3DP

www.bloomsbury.com

9781408192542

A CIP record for this publication is available from the British Library.

10 9 8 7 6 5 4 3 2 1

Typeset by Fakenham Prepress Solutions, Fakenham, Norfolk NR21 8NN
Printed by CPI Group (UK) Ltd, Croydon CR0 4YY

This book is produced using paper that is made from wood grown in managed, sustainable forests. It is natural, renewable and recyclable. The logging and manufacturing processes conform to the environmental regulations of the country of origin.

Praise for *Achievement for All*

'This book is the story of a game changer. The vast transformations that have taken place in the English educational system over the last three decades have done little or nothing for the youngsters who are the core concern of Achievement for All. Achievement for All has changed that conclusion beyond all recognition. By putting together our best knowledge on teaching, learning, leadership and parental engagement and converting it into practical action, the participants in Achievement for All have made huge positive impacts. The book describes the work and offers rich case-study illustrations of the materials, tools, practices and experiences of the participants. This is a 'must-read' for all school leaders. It should be considered a 'must do' for any school leaders who have yet to match the pupil gains shown here.'

Professor Charles Desforges OBE, Parental Engagement Pioneer, former Director of Teaching and Learning Research Programme, Economic and Social Research Council and Deputy Vice-Chancellor, University of Essex.

'Achievement for All is one of the most important current opportunities in education and undoubtedly tackling one of the most crucial current issues, that of ensuring all pupils, including those of lower ability whether or not said to have special educational needs, achieve. This book sets out the successes, in many cases beyond their highest expectations, of the schools that were the brave ones to blaze the trail. The London Borough of Camden took the lead in gathering every school in the borough to take part and was privileged to marvel at the progress made by so many participating schools.'

Tim Coulson, Director of Education and Learning, Essex Local Authority and former Director of Quality, Camden Local Authority.

'This is a highly readable and inspiring story of how committed people can make a real impact, changing lives and changing society. It is a story of success against the odds and shows how you can make a difference with leadership and determination. This is a book for anyone who believes in better.'

Jo Owen, Social Entrepreneur and Author of How to Lead.

'Through strong evidence based research, Achievement for All 3As demonstrates extensive material which can be used to deliver the Achievement for All programme. I have no doubt that the work which Sonia Blandford and Catherine Knowles have carried out will go to on transform the lives of many young SEN learners.'

Graham Allen MP, Chair- Early Intervention Foundation.

'This timely book provides practical, accessible and important information for improving access, aspirations and achievement not only for the 20% of the pupil population in England recognised as SEND, LAC and receiving FSM, but for all children. By capturing the essences of this programme in the form of empirical case studies involving real pupils and schools, the work of Achievement for All 3As and the difference it has made to the lives of pupils and the improvement of the schools are very tangible. This now national programme, starting from humble but ambitious beginnings has led the way in repositioning the emphasis of pupil participation and progress back in the classroom. Yet, the infrastructure of the Achievement for All 3As programme involves much more than an emphasis on teaching and learning; with effective leadership, parental engagement and wider outcomes in education and society key features too. Through a process of monitoring and evaluation, and with the support of dedicated Achievement Coaches, schools now have a real, workable and above all sustainable approach to developing and delivering a programme that has been proven to work. If you want to know how to raise aspirations, improve access and achievement – simply read this book. Your next step would naturally be to register for the programme. I personally look forward to July 2016 when 6,000 schools nationally will be enrolled with Achievement for All 3As.'

Dean West, Teacher, Subject Leader and Liaison & Outreach Manager, King Edward VI College, Stourbridge.

This book is dedicated to all pupils, parents, leaders, teachers and wider professionals engaged in supporting vulnerable and disadvantaged learners.

All royalties received from the sale of this book will be donated to Achievement for All 3As, Charity number 1142154.

Contents

Foreword 1

The current Special Education Needs and Disability (SEND) system has failed too many children with SEND. While the principles that guided the system were good when adhered to, for too many children in too many places we have still been living with the hangover of a system that thought children with SEND were uneducable and could not aspire to achieve and be the best they possibly could. Schools expectations were too low and resources not focused on those with greatest needs. This could be seen in the appalling gap between the achievement for children with SEND and those without; the conflict and friction in the system between parents and professionals and that rising expenditure on SEND had produced almost no discernible impact on parental confidence and children's outcomes. This was the situation I found when I conducted my Inquiry into Parental Confidence in the SEND system.

What was more frustrating was that you could go into two schools of similar size, catchment area, resources and children. In one, children with SEND would be thriving, in the other more or less written off. This happened under the same legislation, guidance and codes of practice. While legislation needed changing it was also clear to me that we also needed a cultural revolution in schools. A revolution that put the best teachers back at the centre of teaching children with the most challenging needs, a revolution in which schools had the aim of ensuring that all children with SEND made progress and attained more and a revolution in which school leaders were measured on the outcomes they achieve for all of their pupils.

There was also another element which needed to be put in place. It is perhaps not surprising if you are asked to look into parental confidence in the SEND system that you would recommend that parents have a bigger voice about that system. The reasons why this is a good idea have been less well understood. While it is a good principle that the parents of children should be listened to, it also has a practical impact on the quality of the service and in improving outcomes and confidence. Parent's involvement in their children's education is fundamental to successful outcomes for their children. This is true for all children but more so for children who have more challenges in their learning. This was established long before my Inquiry and confirmed by every national and international study undertaken in recent years in the UK, America, and the European Union. Further the greater the level of parental involvement with the school the greater the level of confidence in school and the SEND framework. The conclusion was clear; parents need to be involved because you cannot improve the system without them.

The key question was how to bring about that culture shift in schools. Changing the legislative framework helps and the new SEND legislation and changed inspection regime from Ofsted reflects a much greater role for personalised learning and better assessment, parental involvement through the local offer and a focus on outcomes all of which are crucial. But legislation and guidance on its own is not enough. To change the system we needed a means to change the culture and focus of what happens every day in every classroom in every corner of the country.

It was out of this ambition that Achievement for All was born. The aim is clear. We needed a radical shift of focus to ensure that the aspiration for every child with SEND was for them to have better outcomes and attainment. At the time we were often told that this was unrealistic, that children with SEND were doing as well as they could. Out of the need to prove that we could do better and by combining the best of what schools leaders already knew into a new way of working, we could make a profound difference to children's lives. This was not about discovering the educational equivalent of the Higgs Boson but it was about forging a new approach out of the best tools and people available. Forged out of what school leaders were already thinking and doing in different areas of the country and bringing this into a new whole which was more than the sum of its parts.

The Achievement for All concept and pilot was developed under the leadership of Professor Sonia Blandford and her team of school leaders as an early recommendation while the Inquiry was still in progress. It is probably rare in the history of pilot programmes in education for an approach to show such definitive and spectacular results. Working in 450 schools over two years the evaluation showed what many had thought impossible. All the children on the programme outperformed all the comparable SEND cohorts not on the programme. But more than this, 37% in English and 42% in maths outperformed their non-SEND counterparts. If this were not enough, attendance of the SEND cohort improved, parental confidence in the schools rose and schools reported a drop in bullying and increase in wider outcomes.

The approach had focused on the four elements we knew had to change from work on the Inquiry and talking to school leaders, parents and young people. The four elements were: focused leadership within the school on SEND to ensure that children's needs are addressed; the best quality first teaching for all the pupils in the classroom which put teachers back in control of children's learning; ensuring parents are fully involved in their children's learning through face to face contact – something the Inquiry had found parents really valued; and ensuring that children and young people are fully engaged in all the school has to offer so they develop the self-confidence to achieve. As the evaluation showed it is not any one or two of these approaches in isolation but the melding and consistent application of all the approaches together which makes the difference.

It is also rare, but perhaps no surprise given the results, that two separate governments have come to the same conclusion about the value of the approach. The incoming government wanted to pick up and move forward with this approach putting additional resources on the table to enable a charity to be set up which could build the infrastructure and develop a national programme that could be implemented in any early years setting, school, college or special school across the country. Further, the approach is now informing how the government is encouraging schools to structure their approach to the new single category of SEND through the indicative code of practice and regulations.

This book is both the story of that journey and the collected wisdom of the school leaders, staff, parents, children and young people who have been on that journey with us. Achievement for All is not something done to schools or parents but in partnership with them. It is just as much the journey of those schools who worked with us on the approach and what they have brought to it.

Achievement for All has been the story of a revolution in our schools. So far a quiet one but growing more noisy and insistent as it becomes ever surer of its ground. The approach has been proved, not just as a pilot but now also as it has been rolled out to over 1,500 schools and growing with results, continuing to prove that it's possible to raise aspiration and achievement in all schools for children and young people with SEND. Too many children, whose futures have been sold short in the past, now have the opportunity to be the best they possibly can, this book shows how and the journey we have been on. I hope that you will take the next stage of it with us.

Brian Lamb OBE, June 2013
Chair of Achievement for All and Chair of the Lamb Inquiry (2008–2009).

Foreword 2

I believe that the Achievement for All programme is one of the most significant developments in special educational needs that we have seen in recent years. It has put ownership of the progress of children and young people with SEND back where it belongs – in the hands of their class and subject teachers. It has tackled the tokenism in the involvement of parents that schools often fall into, and recognised that pupils need to be engaged as well as taught if they are to achieve in school.

Like any other group of children, those with SEND need to feel 'done with' not 'done to'. Achievement for All promotes this 'done with' feeling for staff as well as students. A large part of its success is the way it enables each school to create its own unique pathway, working within an overall framework and vision.

This vision comes through powerfully in this book. 'As practitioners', the authors suggest, 'we should ask the question – if we were to shine a light on every pupil, how many would not be able to make progress? The answer, of course, is none.' The case studies in the book illustrate how outstanding leaders in diverse schools have shone that light, and the profound impact on standards they have seen as a result.

These case studies and the research summaries in this book provide an invaluable resource for other schools embarking on Achievement for All. I know that those schools have made a wise decision in joining the programme. I know they will see a transformation in attitudes and beliefs of staff, pupils alike. And I hope that in their turn they will play their part in supporting other schools who are at the beginning of their Achievement for All journey.

Jean Gross CBE, June 2013
Independent Consultant and former Communication Champion.

Preface

Thank you for choosing to read the first edition of *Achievement for All: Raising Aspirations, Access and Achievement*.

This book has been written to support leaders, teachers, parents, pupils and wider professionals responsible for ensuring that all pupils can achieve through your engagement with Achievement for All 3As and the Achievement for All programme.

In England today, there are too many pupils who are not fulfilling their potential and who are also unhappy at school. Pupils with Special Educational Needs and Disability (SEND), Looked After Children (LAC), pupils eligible for Free School Meals (FSM) and other vulnerable and disadvantaged pupils are most likely to:

- experience various levels of commitment and support from school leaders, teachers and wider professionals
- experience bullying at school
- have poor school attendance
- fail to gain academic qualifications and gain access to further or higher education.

The achievement gap between the 1.5 million (21%) of pupils identified with SEND and those without is as wide as 42% at each key stage and is not closing.

The Lamb Inquiry (2009) exposed failures in the system, parents' frustrations and too great a focus on processes rather than outcomes.

During his inquiry into parental confidence Brian Lamb often discussed with parents the aspirations they had for their children. They told him two things:

- they wanted better outcomes for their children
- they wanted their children to be valued for the contribution they could make.

We know that the effective engagement of parents leads to a profound impact on children's progress and to a mutual trust between parents and schools. When this is absent, outcomes decline and confidence in the school and the SEND system drains away.

We also know that the educational achievement for children with SEND is too low and the gap with their peers too wide. Our failure to give children with SEND the same chance to reach their potential as other children represents a huge loss of talent and society ends up footing the bill. This tragic failure to realise children's potential and parents' aspirations has gone on too long.

We need a system which values children with SEND.

- A system that encourages aspiration and provides children with the support to achieve better outcomes, helping them strive to be the best they can be.
- A system that welcomes parents as valued partners in improving outcomes for their children.
- A system that values children with SEND, ensuring that they are welcome and happy members of their school community.

Out of this desire to ensure that children with SEND are not failed in the future Achievement for All was born.

The Achievement for All programme

In his inquiry Brian Lamb recommended the creation of the Achievement for All programme; a national programme designed to meet the learning needs of children identified with SEND. In 2013 this was extended to include LAC and those receiving FSM. Achievement for All is based on the belief that school leaders, teachers and support teachers can have a profound impact on all children by raising their aspirations and achievements and improving their access to learning.

The Lamb Inquiry (DCSF, 2009) marked a turning point for SEND, placing it more firmly within the domain of school leadership and bringing greater focus to inclusive education. In 2008, Lamb was commissioned to make recommendations on how provision could be improved for SEND learners. His core recommendations included changing the way SEND is identified, making schools more accountable for the progress of low achieving learners and supporting schools in setting high aspirations for all, focusing on attainment, engaging parents and developing wider outcomes. These recommendations are embodied by the Achievement for All programme.

During the pilot (2009–2011) the programme was further endorsed in the SEND Green Paper – *Support and Aspiration: A new approach to special educational needs and disability* (DfE, 2011), which acknowledged it as an effective means of enabling children with SEND to achieve 'better educational outcomes and accelerated progress'. The document outlined proposals for a cultural change including personalised budgets for parents/carers, a new Education, Health and Care plan (replacing Statements) and a single assessment process, replacing School Action and School Action Plus.

The report that summarised the responses to the Green Paper, *Support and Aspiration: A new approach to special educational needs and disability – progress and next steps* (DfE, 2012) recommended the national roll-out of the Achievement for All programme 'to ensure schools have access to what works well'. The document also emphasised the centrality of picking up children's needs early, giving headteachers the opportunity to develop their knowledge and skills to get the best outcomes for all children and putting measures in place to prevent the 'over-identification' of SEND in schools. The document emphasised the new focus on outcomes rather than processes in the identification of children with SEND and an assurance that 'pupils' needs are not missed'. The new focus on inclusive schooling is clear and changes are being legislated through the Children and Families Bill, announced in the Queen's speech in May 2013. Draft legislation on reform of provision for children and young people with SEND, was presented to parliament in September 2012 by the Secretary of State for Education, outlining a birth–25 years single assessment for Education, Health and Social Care to replace the Statement of SEN, personal budgets for parents and carers, a local offer and greater co-operation between services around the child.

The revised Code of Practice planned for 2014, will provide 'clear guidance on identifying children who have SEN and on the operation of a new single category of SEN. Supporting documentation to the Children and Families Bill affirmed the government's intention to ensure that the code of practice 'will reflect the key features' of the Achievement for All approach (TSO, 2013).

The Achievement for All programme has bridged two governments and continues to deliver high quality, high impact outcomes for vulnerable and disadvantaged pupils and those identified with SEND.

Achievement for All 3As

Achievement for All 3As is a registered charity, founded and led by Professor Sonia Blandford since 2011. In the same year the charity won a competitive tender to lead the national roll out of the Achievement for All programme. Based on a similar model to that of the pilot that ran from 2009–2011 in 454 schools across England and was also led by Professor Sonia Blandford, the current programme is demonstrating a huge impact on the achievement (literacy and mathematics) of vulnerable learners.

Our mission

To transform the lives of vulnerable children, young people and their families, including those with SEND, by raising their educational aspirations, access and achievement.

Our vision

Achievement for all: a world in which all vulnerable children and young people can develop their skills, interests and capabilities to achieve.

Reaching all children: the pupil premium

Since April 2011, schools have received extra funding for pupils claiming FSM (including those registered at any time in the previous six years) and LAC. Ofsted is clear: schools are accountable for the progress and attainment of these vulnerable learners, with quantifiable outcomes. The particular focus of the Achievement for All programme has been very effective in supporting schools to maximise the outcomes for the most disadvantaged. Government data highlights the intersection of characteristics shared by this group of learners; pupils claiming FSM and LAC are more likely to be identified with SEND.

The impact of Achievement for All to date has been profound. In the 2009–2011 pilot the University of Manchester independent evaluation found that:

- 37% of pupils with SEND achieved or exceeded expected levels of progress in English compared to ALL pupils nationally.
- 42% of pupils with SEND achieved or exceeded expected levels of progress in maths compared to all pupils nationally.
- There was a 10% drop in persistent absenteeism.
- The number of Achievement for All schools reporting excellent relationships with parents increased by 36%.

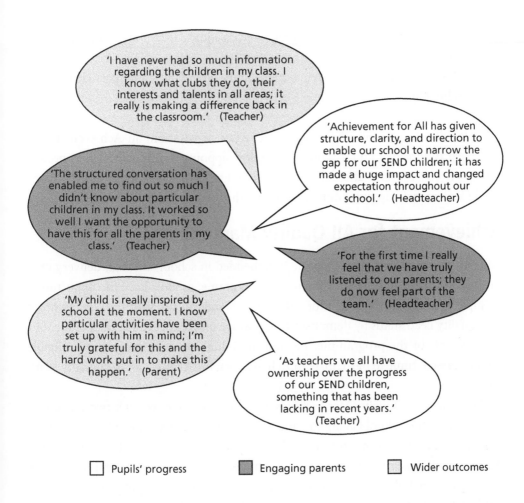

'I have never had so much information regarding the children in my class. I know what clubs they do, their interests and talents in all areas; it really is making a difference back in the classroom.' (Teacher)

'Achievement for All has given structure, clarity, and direction to enable our school to narrow the gap for our SEND children; it has made a huge impact and changed expectation throughout our school.' (Headteacher)

'The structured conversation has enabled me to find out so much I didn't know about particular children in my class. It worked so well I want the opportunity to have this for all the parents in my class.' (Teacher)

'For the first time I really feel that we have truly listened to our parents; they do now feel part of the team.' (Headteacher)

'My child is really inspired by school at the moment. I know particular activities have been set up with him in mind; I'm truly grateful for this and the hard work put in to make this happen.' (Parent)

'As teachers we all have ownership over the progress of our SEND children, something that has been lacking in recent years.' (Teacher)

☐ Pupils' progress   ▦ Engaging parents   ☐ Wider outcomes

Results from the pilot have also been replicated in the first year of the national roll out of the programme. Some of the comments made by school leaders, teachers and parents are shown in the diagram above.

The Achievement for All programme

The Achievement for All programme is delivered in partnership with schools across England – primary, secondary, special schools and pupil referral units (PRUs) – and provides a bespoke framework for school improvement. Building on current school practices, the framework is operationalised through the four key elements of:

1 Leadership of school, classroom and teams; teaching and learning.
2 Teaching and learning, assessment and data tracking, planning and delivery.

3 Parental engagement, structured conversations; listening to and engaging with parents.
4 Wider outcomes, improving behaviour; attendance and participation in school life.

Schools self-select to join the programme. After registration, an Achievement for All coach is allocated and a school 'champion' appointed internally. The approach is strongly collaborative and, following an initial needs analysis, areas where change would be beneficial to pupil outcomes across the four elements are identified.

Achievement for All Quality Mark scheme

The Achievement for All programme is embedded in schools through delivery over two years. During and beyond the main programme, schools have the opportunity to implement the Achievement for All Quality Standard, and gain the Quality Mark and Quality Lead status by demonstrating positive outcomes against each of the four key elements of the programme. Beyond the initial two-year programme, eligible schools can continue to participate in Achievement for All through the Quality Mark scheme.

To maintain the Quality Mark schools need to be reaccredited after two years. This is initiated by the School Champion and Achievement Coach who will agree that the school has maintained progress at the level set out in the Quality Mark criteria. The Achievement Coach will then make a recommendation to Achievement for All 3As and a panel including representatives of the charity trustees, programme leaders, headteachers and an independent member will decide whether or not to reissue the award. Schools will be required to re-register before the Quality Mark is awarded again.

How the book works

This book is presented in eight chapters, each containing evidence-based research and practice. The aim is to provide the reader with sufficient material to formulate a view that will assist them in the delivery of the Achievement for All programme, supported by an Achievement Coach.

> Throughout the book 'school' is a generic term encompassing primary, secondary, special, PRUs, academies and free schools.

Chapter 1 provides an insight into the thinking, which underpins aspiration, access and achievement, illustrated by the significant outcomes of the Achievement for All schools.

Chapter 2 tackles the longstanding issue of leadership for inclusion. By capturing key research findings and practice the chapter provides the depth of understanding needed to embrace Achievement for All.

Chapter 3 focuses on Element one – Leadership. In providing a clear focus for leading inclusion, the chapter prepares the way for whole-school commitment to all pupils achieving in the classroom and beyond. Case studies serve to illuminate changes to leadership practice when school leaders were challenged by Achievement for All.

Chapter 4 introduces conceptual understanding of Element two – Teaching and learning, an area where there has been significant research since 2000, much of which continues to inform the Achievement for All programme. The examples presented are illustrative of the creativity that exists within the teaching profession and wider community.

Chapter 5 is at the heart of the book and Achievement for All practice. Element three – Parental/carer engagement – this continues to have significant impact on outcomes of pupils identified with SEND, LAC, pupils in receipt of FSM and other vulnerable and disadvantaged pupils. Comments from parents, teachers and leaders serve to emphasise the profound impact of the programme on children and their families.

Chapter 6 extends the development of provision to Element four – Wider outcomes. The impact of the programme on improving behaviour, attendance and participation in community and school life has been well documented, and this chapter provides an insight into the range of activities that provide the motivation for change.

Chapter 7 focuses on monitoring and evaluation, terms that remain understated and undervalued within schools. The chapter aims to provide sufficient guidance that will encourage schools to view monitoring and evaluation as useful tools in identifying and embedding good practice, while saving time.

Chapter 8 looks back over the creation of the charity, Achievement for All 3As, in order to look forward to the many facets of practice that can be developed in partnership with schools and the wider education community.

This book is written to support, not replace, the work of the Achievement for All programme team, who work in partnership with school leaders, teachers, parents, pupils and wider professionals to improve the outcomes for pupils identified with SEND, LAC, pupils receiving FSM and other vulnerable and disadvantaged pupils.

The next stage for your school

In evaluating the Achievement for All pilot, the University of Manchester completed one of the largest studies of a programme for children identified with SEND in Europe. To assist with the next stage of the development and roll-out of the programme they recommended that:

- There should be a strong focus on school-led improvement in order to transform the outcomes for children with SEND. The most successful schools in the pilot had strong leadership from the headteacher or senior leadership team – rather than relying purely on the SEN coordinator (SENCO).
- Teachers should carry out regular target reviews with parents to monitor progress of children and assess where extra help may be required.
- Regular, scheduled conversations on educational outcomes between parents and teachers should take place, with teachers given extra training in managing these relationships.
- Schools should build on existing good practice and share ideas between schools, as this is when the Achievement for All programme is most successful.

For the charity, our priority remains the national roll-out of the Achievement for All programme – to reach up to 6,000 schools by July 2016.

- To achieve this mission we look towards broadening and deepening our work with schools, academy groups and local authorities, extending our engagement across the UK.
- To address the challenge of underperformance of pupils identified with SEND we will extend our reach to include early years.
- To develop our impact and to increase our understanding of each of the four elements we will continue to work in partnership with educational and SEND organisations and extend our partnerships to include parent organisations.

- To increase our understanding of SEND, leadership and schools in challenging circumstances we will pilot programmes overseas.

The authors of this book and the wider Achievement for All community welcome your readership and hope that it will serve to stimulate sufficient interest to embed the Achievement for All programme in the life of your school.

For further information please contact us:
Website: www.afa3as.org.uk
Telephone: 00 44 1635 279 499
Email: sonia.blandford@afa3as.org.uk
        catherine.knowles@afa3as.org.uk.

Acknowledgements

Achievement for All: Raising Aspirations, Access and Achievement would not have been written and published without the support, encouragement and permission to use existing material from a large group of people.

We would like to thank the following Achievement for All schools:

Abbey Hills Primary, Nottinghamshire
Acland Burghley, Camden
Alexandra Park Primary Junior School, Oldham
Badger Hill Primary School, Redcar and Cleveland
Bankwood Community Primary School, Sheffield
Beckers Green, Essex
Bedonwell Infant and Nursey, Bexley
Beeston Fields Primary, Nottinghamshire
Bexley Academy
Birkbeck Primary School, Bexley
Brightlingsea Juniors, Essex
Brightside Infant and Nursery School, Sheffield
Brookside Primary School, Nottinghamshire
Caedmon Primary School, Redcar and Cleveland
Caludon Castle, Coventry
Carlton Central Juniors, Nottinghamshire
Carlton Primary School, Camden
Cashes Green, Gloucestershire
Chosen Hill, Gloucestershire
Cirencester Infants, Gloucestershire
Coundon Court, Coventry
Danson Primary, Bexley
De La Salle Secondary School, Essex
Dormanstown Primary School, Redcar and Cleveland
East Wickham Infants, Bexley
Frederick Bird Primary, Coventry
Grangetown Primary, Redcar and Cleveland

Great Bradford Infants and Nursery, Essex
Hampstead School, Camden
Harbour Primary, Sussex (formerly Grays School)
Huntcliffe Secondary, Redcar and Cleveland
Innsworth, Gloucestershire
Killisick Junior School, Nottingham
Kingsgate, Camden
Kingswood Primary, Gloucestershire
Lee Chapel Primary School, Essex
Lockwood Primary, Redcar and Cleveland
Lyng Hall Specialist Sports College and Community School, Coventry
Newfield School, Sheffield
North Chadderton, Oldham
Oakwood Special School, Bexley
Orchard Primary School, Sidcup
Park Junior School, Gloucestershire
Parliament Primary, Gloucestershire
Primrose Hill Primary, Camden
Radclyffe Primary, Oldham
Redcar Community College, Redcar and Cleveland
Robert Mellors, Nottinghamshire
Roxwell Church of England Primary School, Essex
Rye College, Sussex
Ryedene Community Primary School, South Basildon
Saltburn Primary, Redcar and Cleveland
Savile Park Primary School, Calderdale
Spring Brook Special School, Oldham
St Michael's Church of England Primary School, Camden
Swiss Cottage Special School, Camden
The Park Infant School, Gloucestershire
Tredworth Junior, Gloucestershire
Westwood Primary, Oldham
White Notley, Church of England Primary, Essex
William Read School, Essex
Withington Primary, Gloucestershire

We would like to thank Jean Gross CBE former Children's Communication Champion, adviser to Achievement for All 3As.

In addition, the authors would like to thank the Achievement for All team, Charlie, Bethany and Mia for their patience and support during the writing of the book.

And with thanks to Holly Gardner and her colleagues at Bloomsbury.

The Achievement for All Programme Team (2013)
Achievement Lead North: David McNaught
Achievement Lead South: Sue Briggs
Senior Regional Lead North: Carey Bennet
Senior Regional Lead South: Karen Iles
Regional Leads
Brian Taylor
Garath Jackson
Helen Harrison
Huw Evans
Catherine Nyman
Karen Thomas
Laura Bromberg
Louise Ishani
Michael Reeves
Mike Donovan
Nick Aslett
Philip McElwee
Stephen Armstrong
Tim Kuhles
Charlotte Baker

1 Achievement for All: raising aspirations and improving access in practice

This chapter is in two sections:

1   Why Achievement for All?
2   Aspiration, access and achievement in practice

Introduction – why are aspiration, access and achievement important?

The importance of education is something that is often lost on many of those compulsory school-age pupils participating in the process, particularly the lowest 20% (or more) that do not attain even the basic level of literacy and numeracy needed to gain sustainable employment, a fundamental requirement for economic and social prosperity in this country. For many (not all) of these pupils the impact of their SEND or the social-economic context of their family is a lowering of aspiration by their teachers, parents, school leaders and wider professionals, resulting in limited access to learning and low attainment.

The lack of aspiration and access to learning and the subsequent impact on achievement underpins our education system and is evidenced by the majority of schools in the UK in their failure to address the needs of the disadvantaged (LAC and those in receipt of FSM) and vulnerable and SEND learners. In most schools this is unintended.

Schools annually celebrate examination results that exceed floor targets, boldly claiming significant success if the attainment of GCSE A–Cs or Key Stage level 4s exceed 70% or more. There is rarely any mention or comment of the 20–30% who have failed to reach the basic levels of literacy or numeracy. What are the life chances of the lowest 20%? Those that do not gain English and maths GCSE are higher in number in our prisons and drug centres and in premature deaths.

Digging deeper, the outcomes of the socio-economically disadvantaged are equally challenging, the correlation between low family income and SEND is over 70%. The relationship between family income and low educational achievement has been discussed for generations. Grammar schools were seen to be an early solution, providing access to high levels of achievement for those considered to be academically able regardless of their socio-economic background. However, where selection prevails, for the many who continue to fail their 11+, their home context impacts on their ability to progress on to further and higher education. In response to low academic attainment in primary and secondary schools in England we now have academies, trust and free schools, tasked with 'narrowing the gap', 'closing the gap' and 'raising standards'.

> The Achievement for All framework focuses on the impact of teaching and learning on pupils irrespective of a schools' governance, structure, funding source or admissions policy. Achievement for All 3As works in partnership with local authorities, Academy chains and schools.

WHY ACHIEVEMENT FOR ALL?

It is important for education in this country that we have an educational system where aspiration, access and achievement apply to all learners. All teachers, leaders and support professionals need to conspire to provide a system where the importance of education is understood and valued by all pupils and their parents.

The Achievement for All vision for education is a system that raises the aspirations of all pupils, supported by parents, teachers, leaders and professionals, providing access to schools that inspire, drive and inform learning for all pupils, the outcome being achievement for all.

Underpinning the vision of Achievement for All are the 3As needed to drive practice in schools:

- *Aspiration* encompasses the expectations, beliefs, understanding and capacity of learners to engage fully and positively in the learning process. It is the mind-set that underpins all educational endeavours, whereby practitioners, parents/carers and learners have a shared understanding of that which can be achieved through the setting of goals (short-, medium- and long-term), culminating in the raising of aspirations.

- *Access* has a two-fold meaning. The first is the removal of barriers preventing access to learning; these can be broad or specific, for example low expectations, physiological, social, environmental, educational barriers and more. The second meaning is the provision of education, compulsory, further and higher, and for those who might not have previously perceived education as having any significance or value in their lives.

- *Achievement* is a term that has been devalued by the political drive to 'count' examination results as the single indicator of educational success or attainment. While it is essential that the workforce is literate and numerate, knowing what achievement is, having the self-efficacy to achieve and recognising when this happens is fundamental to learning. Achievement lies within and extends beyond exams: social, artistic, musical, sporting and leadership endeavours all count towards the achievement for all. It is the breadth of success that facilitates the application of learning.

As shown throughout this book, Achievement for All takes a whole-school approach to school improvement, focused on improving teaching and learning for all pupils. The particular focus is on the 20% of the school population identified as having SEND and the vulnerable and disadvantaged, including those receiving FSM and LAC. Too many of these pupils do not achieve as well as their peers relative to their starting points, and are leaving education without the skills and qualifications they need to become independent adults.

Achievement for All is based on the belief that teachers and school leaders can have a profound impact on all pupils and young people by developing their achievement, access and aspirations. This means having high expectations of what pupils can achieve, working in partnership with parents to set targets for learning and track progress, and increasing the range of learning opportunities available to them. While an effective teacher increases access and raises aspirations as a means to improving achievement, an inspirational teacher improves achievement in a way that changes pupils' aspirations, and in doing so improves their life chances by securing access to continued achievement and self-fulfilment.

What next for policy in the UK?

The SEND Green Paper (England, DfE, 2011) moves to the Children and Families Bill, and the government is asking schools to report on the outcomes for the lowest 20%, by raising floor targets. The national roll-out of Achievement for All, supported by the Department for Education, is in place. Policy makers need to join up requirements with practical solutions, using the evidence of impact to secure support from school leaders.

What next for education in the UK?

There will be a change in practice in schools, to one where all pupils are inspired to learn, where there is a shared understanding of the aspirations of all pupils, where barriers to learning are removed and all pupils can achieve.

What next for schools?

The next step across all phases and types of schools in the UK is for school leaders to implement the Achievement for All framework and to adopt the 3As.

A systemic change needs to occur in schools – in the classroom, in support teams and in leadership. Implementing Achievement for All practices builds confidence in raising the achievement, access and aspirations of all learners. The impact is shared outcomes for all vulnerable and disadvantaged pupils and their parents through raising aspirations in every lesson. Confident school leaders and teachers raise the achievement of all pupils through the practice of Achievement for All, which is transferable to learning throughout the school.

The outcome is achievement for all and, for those who are driven by GCSE and Key Stage 2 results, the possibility of 100% success.

ASPIRATION, ACCESS AND ACHIEVEMENT IN PRACTICE

For each of the case studies in the following section, consider what the school has done to increase access and raise aspirations and achievement.

Evidence – aspiration

Aspiration relates to having high expectations about what learners can achieve. It reflects a 'can do' mentality displayed when a pupil decides to meet challenges and gain access to learning, thus believing that they can succeed. Pupils identified with SEND and other disadvantaged learners may reduce their aspirations and consequently become demotivated. Pupils with low aspirations do not always hold their future in high regard and may not have a vision for further education or extra-curricular activities.

The following section breaks down into four key areas to reveal in more detail how Achievement for All has been able to increase the aspirations of pupils with SEND. The areas for focus will be attitudes, parental aspiration, motivation, and school and teacher aspiration.

"...you all have greatness within you."

Henry Winkler: *First News* My Way Achievement for All National Tour 2012

Attitudes

A pupil's mind-set can greatly affect their desire to access school, achieve and improve their future. Pupils can be disengaged or negative for a number of reasons, ranging from established family views about education to their previous experiences in school. Here are some outcomes from schools taking part in the Achievement for All programme relating to students' attitudes.

- Improving access has been shown to challenge negative mind-sets and raise low self-esteem. One school provided pupils with SEND with role models to engage in one-to-one literacy, numeracy and extra-curricular activities. Pupils developed a different outlook towards learning through raised attainment and a willingness to take part in activities, mirrored at home with a more positive attitude towards school and better behaviour around parents. *(Ryedene Community Primary School, South Basildon)*
- Pupil attitudes and relationships altered in one school through a programme of Saturday morning activities. Thanks to community involvement and shared responsibility and enjoyment, families noted a more positive outlook about what their children could achieve. There was a marked improvement in pupils' attitude to school and their relationships with adults also developed. *(Frederick Bird Primary, Coventry)*

Case study: Caludon Castle, Coventry

Context
Caludon Castle is a Business and Enterprise school, which chose their assistant head of inclusion to lead Achievement for All. She worked closely with an English teacher to support development of wider outcomes.

Key challenges
The English teacher had a Year 7 class in which two Achievement for All pupils with social difficulties were identified as needing to become more independent learners. Neither pupil was involved with extra-curricular activities. Pupil A was extremely shy and reluctant to attend school. Pupil B was sociable but lacked confidence and self-awareness.

Approach
The teacher initiated a faculty ambassador programme, starting within English. She recruited for it generally but personally invited the two Achievement for All pupils to volunteer. The planned outcomes for those pupils related to increasing pupil voice, raising enjoyment of school, both in and out of lessons, and boosting independent learning.

The group of eight volunteers met with the teacher every two weeks for approximately half an hour to practise a range of social skills related to specific roles they would be undertaking including:

- meeting and greeting visitors and new pupils
- contributing to curriculum development
- carrying out observations of English lessons to provide feedback

- supporting transition for incoming Year 6 pupils, including supporting a drama performance involving new parents and pupils.

The skills sessions were run by the teacher with occasional involvement from other staff. The teacher was provided with a small budget to purchase badges for ambassadors to wear when in role. Examples of work developed by pupils were shown, as well as photographs.

Outcomes

All ambassadors made vital contributions to changes and there was an increase in requests for group work and peer assessment from pupils.

Pupil A and Pupil B were provided with opportunities to interact with a wider variety of adults and other pupils, enabling them to improve their social and communication skills.

One teacher wrote, 'Subject teachers have noticed an increase in confidence in lessons and report that both are more independent learners. The ambassadors are now involved in coaching other pupils from another local school who are just introducing the initiative.'

Pupil A is willing to be in class and spends less time being taught in isolation. He is less dependent on the support of a teaching assistant (TA) and is managing distractions better. His performance in drama has improved significantly and other pupils have noticed this. As a result he has more enthusiasm for attending school and his enjoyment of learning has increased. He has a sense of purpose thanks to his role as an ambassador. He confidently reports, 'At the start of the year I had no reason to come to school. I didn't like it. But then once I was asked to come into the English ambassadors I got more confident and was coming nearly every day.'

Pupil B has become more aware of herself in social situations. From September to July she exceeded her target grades in English and has since become more reflective as a learner. She feels a sense of pride and responsibility drawn from her position as a faculty ambassador, noting that it makes her feel important as she represents the whole year group in English.

Key learning points

- Start with a small group and include the Achievement for All focus pupils among them to develop inclusion and detract from the stigma of SEND.
- Try to use ambassadors of a previous cohort to support new ones.
- Share the successes of the pupils with other members of staff and parents.

Parental aspiration

Parental engagement has a very distinct and wide-reaching effect on pupil aspirations. Parents with low aspirations often unintentionally pass their beliefs and feelings on to their children. Furthermore, parents who do not understand the education system may struggle to communicate aspirations to their children. Without good modelling of an aspirational outlook, it can be difficult for children to have their own.

- Parental aspirations have been raised through Achievement for All by involving parents in decision-making processes, giving them the opportunity to express their views and aspirations for their child. *(Orchard Primary School, Sidcup)*
- One school found that many parents were unemployed; those that were in paid employment worked night shifts. A high percentage, especially mothers, had little or no expressive English. Raising parental engagement and aspirations was achieved through Achievement for All by providing lifelong learning classes in maths, phonics and reading. Structured conversations were used to signpost other agency involvement and helped to provide support for meetings, housing and benefit discussions. *(Westwood Primary, Oldham)*
- 'Hard to reach' parents may lack information about their child's progress and attainment. Raising parental aspirations was key for one school, as a way to engage pupils with SEND in collaborative relationships and ensure that pupil progress was accelerated. After structured conversations, parents were more aspirational for both themselves and their child, and had an increased awareness of factors that may inhibit their child's learning. *(Tredworth Junior, Gloucestershire)*
- Attendance of parents of pupils with SEND at parents' evenings was often low. Structured conversations were used as a means to set aspirational targets and actions. Parents began to offer suggestions about how they could be more involved with school and support their child. Some have become ambassadors to encourage other parents to be involved in wider school activities. *(Beeston Fields, Nottinghamshire)*

Case study: Redcar Community College, Redcar

Context
Redcar Community College serves an economically challenged area containing the seventh poorest ward in England. This manifests as significantly low levels of literacy, numeracy and especially low self-esteem and aspirations, both among the school population and the wider community.

Key challenges
The school has worked hard to establish good relations with parents and break down barriers between home and school. They have used a variety of initiatives to actively engage parents and carers in their children's learning and to increase aspirations.

Parents lacked understanding of their children's education and found it difficult to support their learning at home.

Approach
Redcar identified a pilot group of Year 7 pupils with SEND who were underperforming in both English and maths. Parents were invited for coffee and an information session alongside their children. They were introduced to shared games, problem-solving exercises and quizzes to encourage positive relationships between parents and their children and between parents and the school to engage their interest.

Sample lessons to show how their children were learning a topic in English or maths allowed parents time and space to ask questions and practise problems with their children. Furthermore, they were encouraged to listen and talk to each other and develop a friendly and supportive relationship with children and teachers. This was developed into a project incorporating research and healthy eating education as well as literacy and numeracy activities.

Outcomes
Parents who completed evaluation forms offered mainly positive feedback. Parents noted how they enjoyed understanding how their children learn and now know what they need to do to help them. Parents developed in confidence; they felt able to ask questions about levels and learning styles, which they would have previously not known about or avoided doing, and trusted staff to answer them. Ofsted interviewed some of this group and reported that relationships between parents and school were outstanding.

Parents have now volunteered to join school activities and willingly attend other school functions, as well as engaging with adult learning opportunities. Three parents have achieved a Level 1 and 2 NVQ Literacy and the current cohort is all taking an ASDAN qualification.

> **Key learning points**
> - Having a clear idea of the programme that the school wants to run is beneficial, but staff must be open to change once the participants' confidence or learning grows so that aspirations can be continually raised.
> - Regular conversations should take place around learning and how children respond to learning opportunities so that parents can understand the direction of their children's aspiration.
> - Project work which integrated literacy, numeracy and ICT skills was the most successful.

Motivation

Motivation relates to the desire to learn and have new experiences and to achieve. Pupil motivation is affected by a number of factors including socio-economic disadvantage and SEND. Motivation in pupils is an aspirational quality as it suggests that the pupils will not only possess a desire to achieve academically but also in the wider context of extra-curricular activities and at home. It is important that pupils with SEND and other disadvantaged learners feel motivated, not only to overcome potential barriers but so that they continue to have aspirations about what they are able to achieve.

- Pupil motivation at home was seen as a common problem. Structured conversations were used to engage pupils to complete homework and raise the quality of that work through personalised development plans. Daily 'good times' diaries reinforced positive attitudes towards being a member of the school community by pupils. *(Carlton Primary, Camden)*
- By taking part in a summer school organised through Achievement for All, parents reported that children felt more motivated to go home and continue with their learning, especially in respect of reading and improving memory skills. *(White Notley, Church of England Primary, Essex)*
- Pupils taking part in Saturday school activities developed an increased motivation to take part in physical activities outside of school and became more likely to take part in school sports, especially if their Achievement for All friends supported them. *(Frederick Bird Primary, Coventry)*
- Structured conversations resulted in parents themselves being more motivated to attend school events, with 100% attendance in structured conversations. Equally, pupils are motivated to access more learning opportunities and improve achievement. *(Westwood Primary, Oldham)*

> **Key learning points**
>
> - Recognise the impact of lack of motivation, self-confidence and self-esteem on pupils' learning.
> - Increased motivation can impact on other areas of the curriculum, such as attitude and behaviour within the class.
> - Try to engender a sense of motivation by giving a child a position of responsibility.

School and teacher aspiration

In order for pupils to become aspirational in the school environment or to continue to raise their aspirations, it is crucial for staff to be aspirational for them. Without a whole-school culture which models aspirational values and holds a strong belief in the pupils' abilities to access and achieve, it is difficult for them to do so.

- In order to tackle a widening gap between the progress of pupils with SEND and other pupils, a team was identified to support each pupil rather than a one-to-one approach. Opportunities to discuss the pupils' progress were identified by the leadership team who encouraged staff to talk and collaborate by sharing their successes or barriers to success. This willingness to talk and help pupils by helping each other shows how their aspirations for these pupils are high, as they continually strive to better their approach to teaching and supporting. *(Robert Mellors, Nottinghamshire)*
- Training staff, to help develop their skills in different areas, revealed an increased willingness to help pupils involved in Achievement for All. Staff were keen to use the strategies learned to increase the aspirations of pupils, concurrently showing that they had raised their aspirations as a school. *(Hampstead School, Camden)*
- Through dedicated Achievement for All training days, the leadership team were able to communicate to staff the action plan and their role within it. In-depth conversations were arranged after this regarding pupils' needs and every member of staff was encouraged to lead or support an Achievement for All activity. It was recognised that sharing the vision so clearly was the major driver for a whole-school commitment. *(Lee Chapel, Essex)*
- A dedicated Achievement for All board was created for staff, showing the leadership structure of Achievement for All, together with pupils' case files and targets, reviews, training, the strand-by-strand school vision and feedback,

creating opportunities for professional communication among staff which leaders encouraged. A 'thought wall' was also put up in the staffroom to encourage staff to share ideas. These ideas were discussed at senior management meetings to ensure the collective voice was heard and implemented in planning ways forward. Through the 'thought wall' all staff were engaged in thinking about improving behaviour in the playground. *(St Michael's, Camden)*

Case study: Beeston Fields Primary, Nottinghamshire

Context
A significant number of pupils in this school are identified as having difficulties with literacy at School Action Plus. The school felt it needed to review the nature of its interventions so that staff were able to support pupils more effectively.

Key challenges
The school lacked a depth of knowledge on individual pupils with literacy difficulties and needed to improve this to enable their needs to be met more effectively, with a specific focus on appropriate interventions for individuals and setting more aspirational targets.

Approach
Structured conversations were held which included an agreed focus between the teacher and the parent about aspirational targets and actions. This gave the meetings purpose and parents saw that the school was interested in their child.

Following the review of the needs of the pupil with the parent, the teacher was able to put an appropriate range of interventions in place to support the pupil more effectively.

This range of new interventions is now rigorously planned and regularly monitored for effectiveness.

Outcomes
The success the pupils have had within reading, writing and maths has raised their self-esteem as demonstrated by improved relationships, attitude to work and general increased confidence.

Achievement for All has led to the school recognising that a culture change needed to take place in the school regarding targets for pupils with SEND. As a result, the teachers now set increased aspirational targets for these pupils and, indeed, all pupils. Achievement for All has led to a whole-school expectation that all pupils should make three sub-levels progress, including those with SEND.

Monitoring and review processes have been introduced and this has also supported the development of aspirational target-setting for pupils with SEND. This is built into the whole-school target as part of teachers' Performance Management.

Key learning points

- The Achievement for All programme can lead to a school culture in which all members have an aspirational outlook for pupils regardless of the barriers they face.
- Whole-school expectations can help improve the progress of individual pupils, especially when these are built into school systems and are part of performance management.

Review questions

- Consider your pupils' aspirations. Do all your pupils have high aspirations for their learning and achievement? How could you raise their aspirations?
- Consider the aspirations you have for the pupils in your classroom. Do you think your aspirations are high for each pupil? How could you raise your aspirations for each pupil? (Consider practical measures.)
- What practical measures could you put in place to better motivate all children? (You might also like to consider this within the context of the saying: success breeds success.)

Conclusion

The Achievement for All programme has been shown to help schools raise aspirations of learners with SEND. By increasing pupil confidence through various initiatives the staff have worked to change mind-sets and attitudes. Parents' aspirations have been raised by sharing their children's achievements and having structured conversations with schools, which allow them to become fully involved in helping their children through education. The stigma associated with pupils with SEND and other disadvantaged learners can be reduced by focusing on whole-school aspirations, so that teachers and leaders become part of and encourage a culture in which all can achieve and progress by setting aspirational targets and having high expectations. By raising pupil, parent and teacher aspirations, schools can also help learners to access opportunities and begin to encourage them to focus on specific areas, such as classroom behaviour, attendance and extra-curricular activities, in order to help pupils gain access to education and feel part of an inclusive culture.

Evidence – access

The Achievement for All programme aims to increase the access all pupils have to learning. The innovative approach it takes in supporting pupils identified with SEND and other disadvantaged learners breaks down the barriers which often prevent them from accessing all the opportunities school has to offer. Many schools have found that the Achievement for All programme has allowed them to improve the access pupils with SEND have to the curriculum – leading to increased enjoyment, greater aspiration and higher levels of achievement. Just as importantly, it has also enabled pupils to access wider outcomes by helping them develop positive relationships and participate in school life.

All schools are now required to provide extended services for the families and communities they serve. Extra-curricular activities allow pupils to develop positive relationships and raise their self-esteem, as well as often leading to improvements in their academic and personal development. However, there is evidence to suggest that pupils identified as having SEND are less likely to take up extra-curricular activities and enjoy these benefits. (Ofsted, 2008)

The Achievement for All programme can help schools improve the extended services and extra-curricular activities they offer to pupils with SEND by:

- Encouraging them to review the provision they offer to pupils with SEND. Schools have found that by using structured conversations with parents *(Beckers Green, Essex)* and pupil surveys *(Roxwell Church of England Primary School, Essex)* to reveal the type of extra-curricular activities pupils would enjoy, they have been able to dramatically improve participation. One school found that empowering SEND pupils to establish and run their own after-school club dramatically improved their confidence and self-esteem. *(William Read School, Essex)*
- Enabling them to target provision at groups of pupils with SEND who need specific support with their academic or social development. After analysing pupil data and engaging parents through structured conversations one school realised that the summer break was proving to be a major disruption in the learning of some pupils *(White Notley, Essex)*. As a result, they put in place an academically based summer school which led to significant improvements in pupil progress the following year.
- Providing greater opportunities for pupils with SEND to form positive relationships with others and integrate into the school community. After

realising that its current provision did not allow for pupils with SEND to represent the school in sports fixtures, one school used Achievement for All funding to establish a *boccia* club specifically for them *(Brookside Primary School, Nottinghamshire)*. Playing against other schools boosted pupil confidence and allowed them to take a lead role in the school community.

- Promoting partnership with outside agencies that can support the school in providing extended services. One school used links with Chelsea Football Club to establish a scheme whereby aspiring players acted as learning mentors for pupils *(Ryedene Community Primary School, South Basildon)*. The support offered to pupils from role models with whom they would not have otherwise come into contact has led to significant improvements in pupils' engagement with school and their academic progress.
- Empowering staff to take on more responsibility for extra-curricular provision. Prompted by its involvement in Achievement for All, one school restructured the way it used its learning support assistants (LSA) so that each took on a new activity to support pupils with SEND *(Lee Chapel Primary, Essex)*. LSAs at the school now take the lead in providing extended services before, during and after school.

Parental engagement

Research shows that parental engagement is a critical factor in achieving positive outcomes for pupils. Without full engagement from their parents, children may lack the support they need to access learning opportunities at home and at school. However, communication with schools can feel like a 'one-way' conversation for parents, leaving them unsure of their child's progress in school and unaware of what they can do to improve it.

The Achievement for All programme allows schools to engage parents in their children's learning by:

- Providing a framework for in-depth discussion through structured conversations. These require an active role to be taken by both parties and have proved successful in engaging 'hard to reach' parents, even where other strategies have failed. *(Brightlingsea Juniors, Essex)*
- Revealing barriers to learning of which they may have been unaware. Fuller dialogue with parents allows more open and trusting relationships to be developed with teachers and more investment in their child's learning *(Carlton*

Primary, Camden). Frequent contact with school allows parents to feel better informed about their children's learning and more confident in supporting it. *(Swiss Cottage Special School, Camden)*

- Offering flexibility in where and when schools engage parents through structured conversations. Many schools have found that this has allowed them to engage with parents who were previously unable or unwilling to do so. *(Radclyffe Primary, Oldham/Cirencester Infants, Gloucestershire)*

- Enabling contact with the school to become more personal and informal. Many schools have found that structured conversations are a more effective way of communicating with 'hard to reach' parents than traditional arrangements *(Lockwood Primary, Redcar and Cleveland/The Park Infant School, Gloucestershire).* Their success has led one school to abandon parents' evenings in favour of days dedicated to holding structured conversations with all parents. *(Westwood Primary, Oldham)*

- Supporting schools in taking innovative approaches to engaging parents. One school found that schemes such as adult learning, cookery classes and parenting skills sessions brought parents into school, including those who had never come before *(Tredworth Junior, Gloucestershire).* Others have involved parents by bringing them into school to observe and support their child's learning directly. *(Grangetown Primary, Redcar and Cleveland/ Kingswood Primary, Gloucestershire/Redcar Community College, Redcar and Cleveland)*

Case study: Dormanstown Primary School, Redcar and Cleveland

Context
Dormanstown Primary School serves a community which experiences significant disadvantage. Some of the challenges that face families have a significant impact upon the well-being of their children and upon their children's ability to access learning.

Key challenges
Many of the pupils with SEND are transported to school in minibuses and establishing quality relationships with their parents can be challenging as the normal contact at the beginning and end of the day does not happen. During structured conversations, parents requested support in motivating their children at home, helping their academic progress and improving their behaviour. Many were keen to support their children but were not entirely sure how they could do so. Some parents perceived themselves as having poor literacy and numeracy skills and were concerned that they may not be able

to help their child. Many also had negative experiences when at schools themselves and felt concerned about coming into school.

Approach

The staff decided to create a whole-school project based around the story of *Alice in Wonderland*. This enabled all pupils and parents to be involved, not just the pupils from the Achievement for All project. Staff worked in teams to develop the project for their classes/key stages and included parent engagement activities within their plans. All sessions involving parents enabled teachers to model to parents how to praise pupils in relation to their targets.

Year 5 and 6 organised visits to the local art college to design and make hats and create a model of the Jabberwocky, with parents invited to these sessions too. Key Stage 2 SEND classes created a café area and worked on designing and cooking food for it. Parents were invited to attend these sessions and were able to have a drink and something to eat, served by the pupils. At the end of the project all parents were invited to a 'Mad Hatter's Tea Party' to celebrate its successes with their children.

Impact

Parents reported that they were keen to attend sessions in school and that they were now clearer about how to support their children. Parents have asked staff what the next project will be and when they can come into school again. Staff have become enthusiastic about inviting parents to sessions in school. Pupils have said they like having their parents in school to help them and that their parents are better at helping them at home.

Developing positive relationships with others

All young people have the right to enjoy school. The extent to which pupils can develop positive relationships with those around them is a crucial factor in determining whether they do so. For LAC the situation can be compounded by frequent change of school. Pupils identified with SEND may struggle to make and maintain positive relationships if they have not yet developed the social, cognitive and linguistic skills required. Evidence also suggests that pupils identified with SEND are more likely to be bullied than their peers (National Autistic Society and Mencap). This can be compounded by the fact that, owing to their needs, pupils with SEND may find it harder to report that they are being bullied. (DCSF, 2008)

Achievement for All can help pupils with SEND to develop positive relationships by:

- Involving pupils, parents and staff in the process of identifying challenges and setting targets to address them. Schools have found that forming positive relationships through structured conversations has led to improvements across school life for a child *(Lockwood Primary, Redcar and Cleveland/ Cashes Green, Gloucestershire/Innsworth, Gloucestershire)*. Having access to a 'common language', shared by their parents and teachers, encourages pupils to take ownership of their development and gain greater self-esteem. *(Kingsgate, Camden/Central Juniors, Nottinghamshire)*
- Helping schools diagnose what may be causing pupils to have negative feelings towards school and others. Pupil surveys in one school indicated that one year group had a particular issue with self-esteem and well-being. This resulted in the school putting in place a range of interventions to support the pupils involved and improve their attitude. *(Kingsgate Primary, Camden)*
- Offering opportunities for teachers and support staff to learn new strategies for promoting positive relationships in school. One school was able to release a teacher to attend training on Social and Emotional Aspects of Learning, who then passed this on through an INSET session. This has enabled the school to offer improved support to a group of pupils it had identified as being particularly emotionally vulnerable. *(Withington Primary, Gloucestershire)*
- Providing new opportunities for pupils to form positive relationships through extra-curricular activities. By establishing a faculty ambassador's scheme for pupils with social difficulties, one school was able to dramatically improve the children's confidence and relationship skills. Giving the pupils this responsibility both improved their self-esteem and gave them the chance to interact positively with staff, pupils and parents. *(Caludon Castle, Coventry)*
- Enabling schools to be better informed about bullying and to take more decisive action on this. Regarding a pupil who was at severe risk of bullying, one school commented that, 'The Achievement for All project has created a really supportive communication framework, whereby key information about pupils such as Pupil X are effectively shared; this allows the school to maximise the impact of any programme of intervention.' *(Acland Burghley, Camden)*

Case study: Saltburn Primary, Redcar and Cleveland

Context

Saltburn has approximately 450 pupils aged 3–11 on roll; 13% of them were identified with SEND. Structured conversations with parents showed that self-esteem and poor comprehension skills were an issue for many pupils with SEND. This case study focuses on one of these pupils, Pupil M.

Key challenges

Pupil M had a history of disruptive behaviour and found it difficult to focus on a given task and listen to instructions. He had low self-esteem and found it difficult to develop new relationships with other children, meaning he had only a small group of friends. Pupil M had low levels of achievement in literacy and was a reluctant reader.

Approach

Structured conversations with Pupil M's mother identified his difficulty in focusing and concentrating on literacy targets. However, the conversation also revealed that he enjoyed reading to and supporting his much younger brother.

It was agreed that Pupil M would become a reading mentor to pupils in Year 3 as a confidence builder and a way of reinforcing his own reading skills. In literacy, Pupil M focused on one target in each lesson.

Impact

Acting as a reading mentor with Year 3 pupils twice weekly had an immediate impact on Pupil M's self-esteem (and the progress of his younger brother as observed by his early years teacher). Pupil M was nervous at first but now thoroughly enjoys the responsibility and is proving to be a very positive and supportive role model.

This enthusiasm has filtered into all other areas of Pupil M's learning and he is more focused and less disruptive in the classroom. Staff now intend to encourage him to listen to others' contributions and ideas as he has so many of his own!

Pupil M's mother feels his attitude to school and learning has improved dramatically and reports that he is leaving school feeling happy and enthusiastic about his day. At the beginning of the year Pupil M was a low achiever with National Curriculum level 2a in reading and writing; this has already moved to a 3c.

Key learning point

- Early planning and organisation of the involvement of parents is a necessity in gaining a full understanding of how pupils can be best supported.

Attendance

Pupils must attend school in order to make progress in their learning. However, research shows that a disproportionate number of pupils identified with SEND (from both mainstream and special schools) and those claiming FSM have poor attendance. The rate of persistent absence among pupils with a Statement of SEN is more than three times the rate among the whole school population; for those claiming FSM, the rate is almost three times. (DfE, 2013)

The Achievement for All programme empowers schools to improve the attendance of pupils. For those identified with SEND this is realised in practice by:

- Encouraging them to reflect on why attendance may be poor and develop specific interventions to improve it. For example, some schools have found that by altering the curriculum to make it more accessible and relevant for pupils, they have been able to engage those who have not previously enjoyed coming to school. *(Abbey Hills Primary, Nottinghamshire)*
- Enabling them to employ dedicated members of staff who can focus on improving attendance and encouraging them to take more innovative strategies to support this. For example, one school was able to take on an attendance officer who used a 'walking bus' scheme to collect pupils at risk of absence from home and bring them in each day. *(Carlton Primary, Camden)*
- Enabling them to improve relationships with parents and the degree to which they encourage their children to attend. Structured conversations allow schools to discover issues which may explain absence from school and engage parents in addressing them. One school found that, by involving parents in this way, they were able to dramatically improve the uptake of extra tutoring for SEND pupils, which had traditionally been low. *(Danson Primary, Bexley)*

Case study: De La Salle Secondary School, Essex

Context
De La Salle has 750 pupils, 11–16 years old, 27% of whom have been identified as having SEND. The proportion of learners known to be claiming FSM is well above the national average.

Key challenges
Two years ago the school was identified as having a problem with persistent absence but has worked robustly to raise attendance, which is now in line with the national average. However, rates of persistent absence among SEND pupils have remained higher than among their peers.

Approach
The lead Achievement for All teacher and the local authority adviser worked together on a tracking and monitoring grid which identified and illustrated attendance, behaviour and attainment data across terms for all identified Achievement for All pupils. This was updated on a weekly basis and anomalies were shared at steering meetings with subject leaders. Data was disseminated to core staff who were able to identify possible barriers to learning in the classroom and address these through personalised learning plans and target setting.

Pupils were rated according to attendance data and parents were informed. Each pupil with attendance below 90% was given a specific target regarding attendance at their first structured conversation and this was monitored closely throughout the year. Pupils' attendance was again reviewed during the summer term and successes were celebrated with parents. Particular focus was placed on pupils whose attendance had not improved or had remained static and this was reviewed as an issue of concern during subsequent structured conversations.

Outcomes
Pupils' expectations have risen. There is now greater access to learning through extra-curricular activities and improved participation in lessons. The number of fixed-term exclusions dropped significantly and the attendance of an identified minority is improving.

By the end of the year the number of pupils in Year 7 identified as having persistent attendance concerns dropped by 50%. In Year 10 the number of pupils in this category dropped by 40% and no other pupils developed concerns over their attendance.

Impact
The action did not have a whole-school impact at first, because it was driven by a small number of teachers and delivered by a single project leader outside the senior leadership team. Many teachers initially thought the action was 'just another gimmick'. The work with Achievement for All became far more powerful when the tracking grid used became a rigorous tool to monitor the progress of individuals and was linked intrinsically to the structured conversations. Staff began to see the project as a catalyst for change, with improved communication that was crucial in improving and sustaining access, aspiration and achievement.

Review questions

- Consider relationships within the school. As a leader, what whole-school measures could you put in place to improve pupil-pupil, pupil-teacher, teacher-teacher and parent-pupil-teacher relationships/interactions?
- As a leader of learning within the classroom, how would you develop and implement a 'zero tolerance' to bullying policy?
- Consider attendance within your school. List some of the ways you could improve attendance at classroom level (class teacher) and school level (senior leader).
- Consider classroom practice. Could you do more to enable every child to access teaching and learning? What could you do to remove learning barriers for the children with SEND and other vulnerable learners? (Consider from both a school leader and class teacher view point.)

Conclusion

The case studies in this section demonstrate the potential Achievement for All has to improve the access pupils with SEND have to both learning opportunities and wider school life. For many schools the programme has offered a chance to reflect on how they approach the issues which can confront these pupils and other vulnerable learners, prompting them to find new and innovative ways of solving them. By improving how they communicate with parents and carers, Achievement for All has also allowed schools to identify previously unknown barriers to learning, leading to greater achievement once they have been broken down. Greater engagement has empowered parents and carers to take an active role in their children's learning, meaning progress becomes more sustainable and schools, parents and pupils hold greater aspirations about what can be achieved.

Summary

This chapter has captured the focus of the Achievement for All programme: nurturing aspirations, increasing access and raising achievement for pupils identified with SEND, LAC and other vulnerable and disadvantaged groups. Research and practice illustrate how the simplest of acts, whether these are communication or pedagogy, can increase participation in learning and enhance the life chances of all pupils.

References

Blandford, S., Tavlos, L., Williams, K., Crowhurst, M. and Knowles, C. (2011), *Achievement for All Anthology, Pilot 2009–2011*, Nottingham: DfE.

Department for Education (2010), *Achievement for All: Interim Report*, Nottingham: DfE.

Department for Education (2011), *Support and Aspiration: A new approach to special educational needs and disability*, Nottingham: DfE.

Department for Education (2012), *Support and Aspiration: A new approach to special educational needs and disability – Progress and next steps*, Nottingham: DfE.

Department for Education (2013), Pupil Absence in Schools in England, including pupil characteristics, 2011/12, SFR, London: DfE.

Department for Children, Schools and Families (2008), *Bullying involving children with special educational needs and disabilities, Safe to learn: embedding anti-bullying work in schools*, Nottingham: DCSF.

Lamb, B. (2009), *Lamb Inquiry: Special educational needs and parental confidence*, Nottingham: DCSF.

NCSL (2011), *Achievement for All: Leadership Matters*, Nottingham: NCSL.

Ofsted (2008), *How well are they doing? The impact of children's centres and extended schools*, London: Ofsted.

The Stationary Office (TSO) (2013), *Children and Families Bill 2013: Contextual Information and Responses to Pre-Legislative Scrutiny*. Presented to Parliament by the Secretary of State for Education by Command of Her Majesty, February: TSO.

2 Learning to be an inclusive school

This chapter is in two sections:

1 Creating an inclusive school
2 The Achievement for All programme in practice

Introduction – the four key elements

The Achievement for All programme, delivered in partnership schools across England – primary, secondary, special schools and PRUs – provides a bespoke framework for school improvement. Building on current school practices, the framework is operationalised through the four key elements of:

1 Leadership of school, classroom and teams; teaching and learning.
2 Teaching and learning – assessment and data tracking, planning and delivery.
3 Parental engagement – structured conversations; listening to parents.
4 Wider outcomes improving behaviour, attendance and participation in school life.

Schools self-select to join the programme. After registration an Achievement for All coach is allocated and a school 'champion' appointed internally. The approach is strongly collaborative and, following an initial gap analysis, areas across the school where change would be beneficial to pupil outcomes, are identified. Target groups are then selected focussing on pupils identified as SEND learners, LAC, those claiming FSM and other vulnerable and disadvantaged groups.

CREATING AN INCLUSIVE SCHOOL

Inclusion acknowledges the impact of the social environment upon children's abilities to learn and develop. It seeks to facilitate diversity and to ensure that pupils' needs are viewed equitably and met fairly (Ainscow, 1999). Founded on the principle of removing barriers to learning and participation (Booth and Ainscow, 2002), inclusive education is most appropriately delineated within a framework for practice; its indistinct boundaries (Ainscow et al., 2004) tend to preclude a precise definition. In practice, inclusive education encompasses such areas as school cultures, policies and practices, child and parental voice and achieving potential (DfES, 2001). The Centre for Studies on Inclusive Education (CSIE) (2011) outlines what this involves in an educational setting:

- Valuing all pupils and staff equally.
- Increasing the participation of pupils in, and reducing their exclusion from, the cultures, curricula and communities of local schools.
- Restructuring the cultures, policies and practices in schools so that they respond to the diversity of pupils in the locality.
- Reducing barriers to learning and participation for all pupils, not only those with impairments or those who are categorised as 'having special educational needs'.
- Learning from attempts to overcome barriers to the access and participation of particular pupils to make changes for the benefit of pupils more widely.
- Viewing the difference between pupils as resources to support learning, rather than as problems to be overcome.
- Acknowledging the right of pupils to an education in their locality.
- Improving schools for staff as well as for pupils.
- Emphasising the role of schools in building community and developing values, as well as in increasing achievement.
- Fostering mutually sustaining relationships between schools and communities.
- Recognising that inclusion in education is one aspect of inclusion in society.

The movement towards inclusive education has been a global phenomenon as demonstrated in the fundamental philosophy and key practice of the United Nations Children's Fund (UNICEF) and the United Nations Education, Science and Cultural Organization (UNESCO, 1994, 2005); UK government policy has promoted inclusive education since the Warnock Report (HMSO,1978). Ruijs et al. (2010: 352), reflecting the Salamanca Agreement (UNESCO, 1994), broadly define inclusive education as the education of children with SEND in a 'regular' school instead of a special school.

The introduction of the Code of Practice (1994) in England, although aimed at helping educators and other stakeholders to identify and assess SEND led to much confusion as to how this could be appropriately carried out in schools (Gibson and Blandford, 2005). In the following decade, related government documentation articulated an indefinite framework, leaving much open to interpretation at the local level; this included inconsistencies in terminology around a definition of SEND and in its assessment.

The Lamb Inquiry (DCSF, 2009) marked a turning point for SEND, placing it more firmly within the domain of school leadership and bringing greater focus to inclusive education. In 2008, Lamb was commissioned to make recommendations on how provision could be improved for SEND learners. His core recommendations included changing the way SEND is identified, making schools more accountable for the progress of low-achieving learners and supporting schools in setting high aspirations for all, focusing on attainment, engaging parents and developing wider outcomes. The recommendations are embodied by the Achievement for All programme. The programme was further endorsed by the SEND Green Paper – *Support and Aspiration: A new approach to special educational needs and disability* (DfE, 2011), which acknowledged it as an effective means of enabling children with SEND to achieve 'better educational outcomes and accelerated progress'. The document outlined proposals for a cultural change including personalised budgets for parents/carers, a new Education, Health and Care plan (replacing Statements) and a single assessment process, replacing School Action and School Action Plus.

Support and Aspiration: A new approach to special educational needs and disability – Progress and next steps (DfE, 2012) recommended the national roll-out of the programme 'to ensure schools have access to what works well'. The document also emphasised the centrality of picking up children's needs early, giving headteachers opportunity to develop their knowledge and skills to get the best outcomes for all children and putting measures in place to prevent the 'over-identification' of SEND in schools. The document emphasised the new focus on outcomes rather than processes in the identification of children with SEND and an assurance that 'pupils' needs are not missed. The revised Code of Practice (2014) will provide 'clear guidance on identifying children who have SEN and on the operation of a new single category of SEN'; the new focus on inclusive schooling is clear and changes are being legislated through the Children and Families Bill (2013).

Increasing access and removing barriers

Government statistics are clear. In 2012, 36% of pupils claiming FSM achieved the standard five or more GCSEs at Grade A*–C compared to 63% of all other pupils. For young people identified as SEND, this figure was 22%. For those whose primary need was behavioural, emotional and social difficulties (BESD – the largest group of SEND primary need at Key Stage 4), less than 18% achieved the standard GCSE expectation including English and maths (DfE, 2013). In addition, children with SEND are more likely to be bullied by their peers and to be excluded from school; in 2011 pupils with a Statement of SEN were nine times more likely to be permanently excluded from school than their peers (DfE, 2012). Sadly there is a big overlap between those with SEND, those receiving FSM and LAC; in 2011 73% of LAC were identified as SEND. Disengagement from school is an inevitable consequence, and children with SEND are more likely to become NEET (not in education, employment or training). In June 2012, 968,000 16–24 year olds were in this category, accounting for 16% of all 16–24 year olds nationally. For those with SEND the situation can be worse: in 2012, government data showed that 30% of 16 year olds with a Statement of SEN were NEETs by the time they were 18 (House of Commons, 2012).

A recent review of the curriculum and qualification needs of young people who are at risk of disengagement suggests, among other issues, that curriculum and qualifications must be relevant to all learners, with 'positive teaching approaches' adapted to learner needs, learning environments which are supportive and less formal and 'supportive relationships' with teachers (Bielby et al., 2012). The important role of the school in enabling pupils to access education is further supported by findings from a YouGov survey for the Prince's Trust (2012). Findings showed that 38% of a sample of over 2,000 young people who left school with no or poor qualifications felt that they did not receive the support they needed at school in comparison to those with better qualifications (21%). *After the Riots*, the final report of The Riots Communities and Victims Panel (2012) cited 'poor parenting' and lack of 'support' and 'opportunity' for young people as primary contributors to the disorder across England in August 2011. Many of those involved in the riots had a history of poor academic performance; 66% of those brought before the courts had been identified as SEND and almost 36% had at least one fixed exclusion during 2009–2010 (Ministry of Justice, 2011).

The Achievement for All programme works with schools, to increase the access all pupils have to learning. The approach it takes in supporting pupils identified with

SEND and other vulnerable groups breaks down the barriers which can prevent them from accessing all the opportunities school has to offer. Schools have found that Achievement for All has allowed them to improve the access pupils with SEND have to the curriculum – leading to increased enjoyment, greater aspiration and higher levels of achievement. Just as importantly, it has also enabled pupils to access wider outcomes by helping them develop positive relationships and participate in school life.

Behaviour

Behaviour is an essential factor in determining how pupils make progress in their learning and access the wider opportunities of school life. However, the 'intricate and profound' link between behavioural standards and SEND (Steer, 2009) means these pupils may find it harder to achieve appropriate behaviour for learning.

Achievement for All has worked in partnership with schools to improve the behaviour of pupils identified with SEND. The following examples provide some insight into how this has been achieved:

- Helping them to identify why pupils may be displaying BESD. By training staff in the use of a new diagnostic tool, one school restructured the support it offered to pupils and greatly improved their behavioural outcomes as a result. *(Great Bradford Infants and Nursery, Essex)*
- Encouraging them to set targets for pupils which take a more holistic approach to their progress in school. One special school (BESD pupils) found that by gaining a fuller picture of pupils' needs they were able to prioritise the actions which would best support their learning. By putting in place interventions which addressed pupils' emotional needs first, they enabled pupils to make much more rapid academic progress than before. *(Oakwood Special School, Bexley)*
- Developing teams which work around the needs of individual children and use multi-agency partnership. *(East Wickham Infants, Bexley)*
- The adoption of Achievement for All prompted one school to redefine the role of support staff and how they supported pupils and their families. By focusing on a caseload of students, 'associate teachers' were able to link together home, school and external agencies in a way that ensured they could provide whatever assistance was needed. *(Lyng Hall, Coventry)*
- Providing them with opportunities to train staff in new strategies for managing poor behaviour and the time/space for this to be put into place. By training

staff in how to develop social skills and resolve adult attachment issues, one school was able to dramatically reduce the number of times children 'opted out' of classroom activities each day. *(Primrose Hill Primary, Camden)*

- Improving the way that they engage parents with their children's behavioural issues. Structured conversations often reveal issues at home which may affect behaviour in school and offer a chance to work with parents in addressing these. *(Parliament Primary, Gloucestershire)*
- Schools have set 'home targets' to promote positive behaviour at home *(Bedonwell Infant and Nursey, Bexley)* and have offered parents training in child care to ensure this is reinforced. *(Park Junior School, Gloucestershire)*

Creating and implementing an inclusion policy

As with professional development, an inclusion/SEND policy will be linked to a School Improvement Plan (SIP). The inclusion policy will relate clearly to the school's vision and be central to school leadership by involving all teachers in the process of identifying its aims and objectives. The implementation plan should also identify with other school initiatives. All policies need to reflect school, local authority, academy group and government policies. The main purpose of any plan should be to improve the quality of teaching and learning for all pupils.

Leaders need to consider how SEND contributes to the development of a learning environment for a community of learners. A fundamental element of learning and teaching is the self-esteem of the pupils, teachers and senior leadership team. Without self-esteem, pupils and teachers will not function in the school community. There is a need for every school to have an inclusion/SEND policy that focuses on personal development and growth. Busher (2000, p. 52) underlines the importance 'in creating an inclusive school, of developing staff abilities to improve the quality of learning opportunities students have'. An inclusion/SEND policy should reflect the ethos of the school and contribute to the fulfillment of its mission.

As with SIPs, an inclusion/SEND policy will reflect the values and beliefs of the school community. It should also relate to the social development of pupils as appropriate to their age and personal needs. Each school will need to have a view on what they particularly wish to encourage; but all schools will need to foster the development of desirable attitudes and personal qualities which can relate to the knowledge and understanding, skills and abilities of the members of their community.

Schools complement and extend the functions of the home and wider community by helping to prepare all pupils to live in society. Pupils need to learn the obligations that go with membership of a group and a community. The development of personal values is an outcome of an effective inclusion policy that relates to the social function of each school. Pupils also need to become aware of their own identity as individuals and of the importance of taking account of the feelings and wishes of others.

In practice, teachers provide a range of opportunities for pupils to learn and develop social skills and attitudes. The process of social development is continued throughout primary and secondary education, in school rules and codes of practice, in school councils and clubs and in the encouragement of pupils' responsibility for themselves and others.

Teachers will benefit from a clear and agreed inclusion/SEND policy that has expectations of them as practitioners. Effective teachers operating under clearly understood guidelines feel confident when giving instructions and are able to develop targets for pupils and teachers.

What makes a good inclusion/SEND policy?

The precise content of an inclusion/SEND policy must be determined by the school community. The recommendations from the DfES (2001a) indicate that whole-school SEND policies are based on a clear set of principles and values. There is a huge difference between simply having an inclusion/SEND policy on paper and having one that actually works well in practice. Some factors that go towards making a policy work are when the policy is:

- Not just a paper exercise, but is used effectively on a daily basis and across the whole school.
- Created in consultation with teachers and pupils.
- Reviewed and updated to ensure that any parts which do not work are altered.
- Clear to pupils, parents and staff.
- A clear and effective part of the whole-school ethos.
- One that puts the emphasis on positive aspects.
- One which lets teachers know what to do, and who to turn to if additional help is needed.
- One which encourages consistency, but also allows for individual approaches to SEND.

In practice, an inclusion/SEND policy will be a comprehensive and assertive statement intended to guide the school community (Johnson et al., 1994). The policy will be the outcome of a democratic decision-making process involving all members of the school community; participation is the key to an effective policy. Senior leaders might begin the process of developing a policy by:

- Identifying the stages of development.
- Identifying key personnel: SENCO and SEND team responsible for writing the policy.
- Deciding on a timescale for short-, medium- and long-term objectives.
- Identifying achievable outcomes related to the school vision and development plan.
- Identifying professional development support and INSET needs for the whole staff.

THE ACHIEVEMENT FOR ALL PROGRAMME IN PRACTICE

The following case study is an interview with the headteacher of an Achievement for All school. In it he outlines what inclusion means to the school, teachers, parents and pupils.

Case study: Lyng Hall School, Coventry
Context
Lyng Hall is an Achievement for All Quality Mark Specialist Sports College and Community School. Situated in Coventry, it has 700 students on roll, but has the highest pupil and staff turnover in the city. Attendance is still an issue for the school, especially for pupils identified as SEND. The school is a church school. The proportion of pupils claiming FSM and those identified as SEND is above average; an above average number of pupils have a Statement. Approximately 30% of pupils at the school have English as an Additional Language (EAL), with 38 languages represented.

An interview with the headteacher

What does SEND mean to you?
We needed a significant redefinition at Lyng Hall. The SEND register is now only for those with a medical or diagnosable cognitive condition. SEND should not be

used to describe issues with behaviour, attendance, underperformance or lack of progress.

What sort of issues has involvement with Achievement for All highlighted and how have you dealt with those?

Achievement for All triggered off a series of questions for us:

- What is the point of the SEND register?
- What is the impact of the Individual Education Plans?
- What are the real barriers to learning?
- To what extent should school take responsibility for the barriers to learning that are attributable to influences outside school?

What does it mean to you to be an inclusive school?

Being an inclusive school means that all pupils are making better than expected progress. We use data to help children who need staff to change the curriculum for them so they are taught exactly what they need, to allow them to achieve their full potential. In my opinion, using current progress trajectories to decide our expectations for pupil progress and exam performance or learning outcomes is dangerous if those expectations are based on the children's rate of progress when they are underachieving.

Take my sixth form results. Last year, 35 children (28% of the total) were accepted by university; yet years ago, when teachers predicted their grades, half of the sixth form had 0% chance of five GCSEs, let alone A levels.

Has Achievement for All helped with strategic planning?

Yes, we now use planning to focus on outcomes for specific groups or individuals. The 'one size fits all' policy is no longer used.

We are strategically more flexible, and we have to be in order to make sure we provide for each individual child. Our motto is 'Whatever it takes!'

We need a very flexible curriculum if we are going to put the children before the policy or the system. Our system of 15 associate teachers is key to ensuring the children come to their lessons, ready and able to learn well. They help the children access the many opportunities available in the school.

Were there any problems?

The main problem was making staff appreciate the value in taking on the problems of the parents. I also worried about my staff's workload but, in a recent Occupational Health Survey, there were no areas of significant stress. The teachers don't mind the hard work I ask them to do, because they can see the effect their actions are having on the lives of the pupils.

How did you communicate Achievement for All within the school?

My senior leadership team has Achievement for All in their job descriptions so it is allied to staff development and performance management. I have a deputy head who ensures the quality of teaching and learning and another who looks after the wider outcomes, such as behaviour and attendance. My heads of department embed Achievement for All in their departmental practice and it is always on the agenda of staff meetings.

With the learning you now have, are there things you would tackle differently?
No. It was huge risk but it has been worth it. The Achievement for All journey has also given me supportive evidence for the recent Ofsted inspection. I also gave the inspectors the Fischer Family Trust data. I keep a detailed portfolio of spiritual, moral, social and cultural evidence, with photos etc., and my self-evaluation form also provided evidence.

Review questions

- What has the school done to become more inclusive? List the changes from the outset to the outcomes.
- In the context of your school, list the changes you would make to become more inclusive.

Summary

Creating an inclusive school involves the coming together of policy and practice. This chapter has demonstrated the methodology required for developing a policy that will result in inclusive practice. As practitioners we should ask the question, 'If we were to shine a light on every pupil, how many would not be able to make progress?' The answer is, of course, none. All pupils have the potential to make progress in school.

References

Ainscow, M. (1999), *Understanding the development of inclusive schools*. London: Falmer Press.

Ainscow, M., Booth, T. and Dyson, A. (2004), Understanding and developing inclusive practices in schools: a collaborative action research network, *International Journal of Inclusive Education*. vol. 8, no. 2: 125–139.

Bielby, G., Judkins, M., O'Donnell, L. and McCrone, T. (2012), *Review of the Curriculum and Qualification Needs of Young People who are at Risk of Disengagement* (NFER Research Programme: From Education to Employment), Slough: NFER.

Booth, A. and Ainscow, M. (2002), *Index for Inclusion*, Bristol: CSIE.

Busher, H. (2000), 'The Subject Leader as a Middle Manager', in Busher, H. and Harris, A. with Wise, C. (2000), *Subject Leadership and School Improvement*, London, Paul Chapman: pp. 105–109.

Department for Education (1994), *Code of Practice on the Identification and Assessment of Special Educational Needs*, London: HMSO.

Department for Education (DfE) (2012), NEET Statistics, Quarterly Brief, Quarter 2: DfE.

Department for Education (2012), Permanent and Fixed Period exclusions from schools and exclusion appeals in England 2010/11: DfE.

Department for Education (2013), GCSE and Equivalent Attainment by Pupil Characteristics in England 2011/12: DfE.

Department for Education and Skills (DfES) (2001), *Inclusive Schooling: Children with Special Educational Needs*, Nottingham, DfES.

Department for Education and Skills (DfES) (2001a), The *Code of Practice for Special Educational Needs*, London: HMSO.

Department for Education (2011), *Support and Aspiration: A new approach to special educational needs and disability*, Nottingham: DfE.

Department for Education (2012), *Support and Aspiration: A new approach to special educational needs and disability – Progress and next steps*, Nottingham: DfE.

Department for Education (2012), *Children with Special Educational Needs: An Analysis 2012*, Nottingham: DfE.

Gibson, S. and Blandford, S. (2005), *Managing Special Educational Needs: A practical guide for primary and secondary schools*, London: Sage.

HMSO (1978), *The Warnock Report*, London: HMSO.

House of Commons Committee of Public Accounts (2012), *Oversight of special education for young people aged 16–25*, London: TSO.

Johnson, B., Whitington, V. and Oswald, M. (1994), 'Teachers' views on school discipline: a theoretical framework', *Cambridge Journal of Education*, Vol. 24, No. 2: pp. 261–276.

Lamb, B. (2009), *Lamb Inquiry: Special educational needs and parental confidence*, DCSF.

Ministry of Justice (2011), *Statistical bulletin on the public disorder of 6th to 9th August 2011–October update*, London: Ministry of Justice.

Prince's Trust (2012), Youth Index, London: Prince's Trust.

Ruijs, N. M., Van der Veen, I. and Peetsma, T. T. D. (2010), 'Inclusive education without special educational needs', *Educational Research*, 52, 4, Dec: pp. 351–390.

The Stationary Office (TSO) (2013), Children and Families Bill: TSO.

Steer (2009), *Learning behaviour: lessons learned. A review of behaviour standards and practices in our schools*, Nottingham: DCSF.

The Riots Communities and Victims Panel (2012), *After the Riots*, the final report of The Riots Communities and Victims Panel, London: The Riots Communities and Victims Panel.

UNESCO (1994), *The Salamanca Statement and Framework for Action on Special Needs Education*. Paris: UNESCO.

UNESCO (2005), *Education for All Global Monitoring Report: The Quality Imperative*. Paris: UNESCO.

3 Leadership of the Achievement for All programme

This chapter is in two sections:

1 Effective leadership – vision and aims
2 Effective leadership of Achievement for All – case studies

Introduction – the key elements of leadership

The Achievement for All programme is based on the belief that school leaders, teachers, and support teachers can have a profound impact on all children by raising their aspirations and achievements and improving their access to learning. The first element within the Achievement for All framework is leadership.

In March 2011 the National College published the findings of a two-year study involving 220 headteachers in focus groups and surveys, which considered leadership in the context of the Achievement for All programme. School leaders agreed that vision, commitment, collaboration and communication were critical to the successful impact of Achievement for All. The leadership element was further developed to ensure that participating schools keep a sharp focus on the achievement, access and aspirations of pupils identified with SEND. The findings have also informed the development of the National College's National Professional Qualification for Headship module, *Leadership for Inclusion: Achievement for All*. The key elements of leadership are:

- **Vision** – A set of core values and beliefs, centred on high expectations for all pupils and positive engagement with parents, staff and other professionals. A wide range of learning opportunities are on offer to the pupils.
- **Commitment** – A commitment to core values, whereby appropriate

opportunities are secured and provided to all pupils, and their progress is tracked. Staff development is supported and promoted.

- **Collaboration** – A culture of collaboration between staff, parents and other organisations. Leaders in and across schools work together with a sense of collective responsibility.
- **Communication** – An ability to communicate effectively, enabling the school community to share in the vision.

What the National College and Ofsted leaders say about Achievement for All

Strong leadership has supported and developed Achievement for All... Achievement for All has had a strong impact on the quality of whole-school leadership.

Maggie Farrar, Acting Chief Executive of the National College (NCSL), Achievement for All Conference, 16 May 2012

Outstanding teaching and learning...should be based on careful analysis of need, close monitoring of each individual's need and a shared perception of the desired outcomes.

Janet Thompson, HMI, National Adviser SEN and Disability, Achievement for All conference, 16 May 2012

Achievement for All has had a profound impact on school performance and outcomes for children and young people. It has demonstrated the importance of whole-school leadership when leading change and improving the provision for vulnerable pupils. In particular, it reinforces the importance of four key attributes of successful leadership – vision, commitment, communication and collaboration. It really is about achievement for all.

Paul Bennett, Director of Primary school Leadership, National College

Research literature

Research literature emphasises the central role of school leaders in shaping inclusive education (Kugelmass, 2003; Kugelmass and Ainscow, 2004). This points towards leadership for inclusion, which is central to the introduction of the Achievement for All programme. Gold et al. (2003: 18) place this within the context of transformational models of leadership (Bass, 1999), characterised by 'inclusivity' and 'teacher participation'. Evidence from a pilot study across 13 schools in Cyprus and exploring inclusion in the context of leadership highlighted the central role of the leader in the development of inclusive education and the place of distributed leadership in developing inclusion (Angelides et al., 2010).

The Achievement for All programme with its particular focus on effective inclusive leadership centered on moral purpose (Fullan, 2007), improved outcomes for children and sustainability, rightly sets it within the wider field of educational leadership; encompassing leading change, building capacity and leading systems (Fullan, 2004). In providing a framework in which leaders, teaching and other school staff consider how to work more effectively with the child as the focus, Achievement for All offers opportunity for leading reform from within (Hopkins, 2009; Carter et al., 2006). That said, the Achievement for All pilot highlighted some schools which already had established inclusive practices. Running parallel to the drive for change across schools is the increased interest in systems leadership (Fullan, 2004). This brings leadership into the broader context of building structures, processes and cultures which act on the system as a whole (O'Leary and Craig, 2007).

Leading the Achievement for All programme in schools is founded on a framework developed by the National College for School Leadership (NCSL, 2009) for the successful leadership and management of SEND. Based on international research in inclusive education (Kugelmass 2003 and Beany 2006) a central theme of the initiative is that of effective leadership practice for SEND provision. The NCSL, a partner in the Achievement for All pilot, engaged with leaders across the participating schools (pilot), to reflect on the characteristics of effective inclusive leadership and their impact on vulnerable learners (Blandford, 2011: 1). At the outset, local authority project leaders worked with schools in examining evidence on identification and outcomes for children with SEND (DCSF, 2009b: 14). This gap analysis enabled schools to identify their key strengths and areas for improvement in developing an Achievement for All implementation plan (DCSF, 2009a: 8).

Gathering evidence

From the launch of the Achievement for All pilot in 2009, the National College commissioned a reference group to analyse, examine and identify learning opportunities for leaders with the core aim of improving inclusive practice within schools.

During the first year of the Achievement for All pilot, six case study schools were selected from a range of phases and regions to capture some of the initial leadership learning. Once selected the case study schools were asked to consider their own priorities, plans and intended outcomes for the introduction of the Achievement for All programme, recognising the specific challenges for leadership and considering what opportunities Achievement for All offered within their particular contexts.

All this has led to a clear understanding of the key leadership characteristics needed to achieve greater inclusion in school.

Leadership during the Achievement for All pilot

The National College research found that leaders within schools implemented, developed and embedded Achievement for All according to their own leadership style within the wider context of the school community. Leadership in participating schools was instrumental in the success of Achievement for All. This was particularly effective in schools which had a focus on inclusive leadership and in those which had incorporated Achievement for All into their SIPs (Blandford, 2010). However, a common issue reflected in the focus group discourse was that of having the time and framework to develop a programme, which was already nascent on many school agendas. Respondents from ten schools cited this as an important aspect in implementing and developing the Achievement for All initiative in their schools. This was also supported by the findings from the evaluation (Manchester University, 2010a: 35) and is reflected in the following comment made by one headteacher during the focus group interviews: 'Achievement for All gave me a national driver to achieve what I wanted to achieve.'

Further findings suggested that where culture and ethos were already founded on inclusive practices, Achievement for All approaches tended to be more focused from the outset. This is reflected in the following example taken from the focus group discussion:

> Achievement for All enabled an affirmation of inclusive practice. We invested heavily in Continuing Professional Development (CPD), which became a whole-school priority. As a vehicle to drive change, Achievement for All enabled us to highlight and challenge the data. We found time to celebrate success, which keeps up the momentum for success.

What leadership lessons did schools learn from Achievement for All?

In providing an overview of leading Achievement for All in schools, school leaders were asked to consider what they had learned about leadership in implementing and developing the programme initiative in their schools. The following diagram illustrates the characteristics of effective inclusive leadership, as determined by Achievement for All.

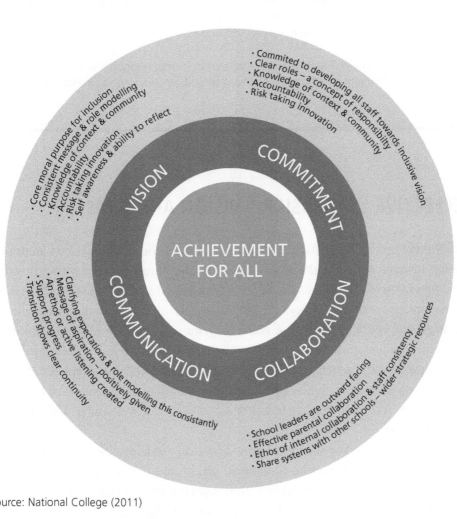

Source: National College (2011)

Effective inclusive leadership is supported by the Achievement for All framework and is founded on:

- A strong **vision** for ALL pupils, supported in equal measures by **commitment, collaboration and effective communication** with parents, pupils, teachers and leaders.
- **Strong values** demonstrated by the behaviour of staff, governors and pupils.
- **Leadership strategies**, embedding Achievement for All in all classrooms.
- **Professional development** for all leaders, teachers and support practitioners, to engage pupils and parents in learning.
- **A focus** on the achievement, access and aspirations of all pupils.

You may find it helpful to reflect on the behaviours in your leadership team in relation to vision, commitment, collaboration and communication. What are the current strengths and areas for improvement?

EFFECTIVE LEADERSHIP – VISION AND AIMS

A measure of a school's effectiveness is the ability of the staff to work as an organisation towards achieving the school's vision underpinned by a shared set of values and beliefs. A vision embeds the philosophy underlying professional and organisational practice within the school. Vision statements are critical to the effectiveness of strategic and operational plans. A vision moves an organisation forward from where it is now to where it would like to be. A vision would be reflected in the school's aims and organisational practice. Visions are notably achievement-orientated, inspirational and aspirational and, as such, should be shared by all members of the school community, including pupils identified with SEND and vulnerable and disadvantaged learners.

The aims that follow the vision provide a clear sense of direction and purpose. These are a means of creating operational plans: objectives or targets to be met by members of the school community within departments and year teams.

Aims provide measurable goals or targets against which the school and teams can monitor, review and evaluate its effectiveness (see Chapter 7).

Creating the school's vision and aims should be a collaborative process. It is important that:

1 The focus is on pupil learning (the central issue of any school).
2 There is the involvement of all possible participants (including leaders, teachers, parents, pupils and support professionals) to facilitate sharing in the decision-making processes.
3 The associated activities are able to be identified and there are direct and easily understood links provided between them and information about them.
4 Responsibilities for decision-making and activities are identified clearly and lines of accountability can be demonstrated.
5 A means to relate resource allocations of all kinds to learning priorities is provided.
6 Evaluation and review processes are facilitated, with the emphasis on further improving opportunities for students.
7 The documentation is limited to simple, clear statements that can easily be prepared by those involved in their already busy schedules.

Vision

School leaders have the responsibility for collaborating with the school community in the generation of its vision. This emphasises a collegial approach to writing and achieving a vision; as each school's ethos is distinctive, school vision or mission statements will also be distinctive, based on shared values and beliefs that manifest themselves in shared practices.

Although management literature emphasises the need for vision in organisations, vision is often an intangible, difficult and ambiguous concept. Fidler (2002. p. 105) describes vision as:

> ...the creative 'double-loop' thinking of trying to envisage how things might be different in the future. It leaps the present and the short term. It looks 10–15 years ahead, sufficient time that things might change radically, and tries to vision the organisation in a new and successful future...the vision is not just a projection forward of the present but it does bear some relation to the starting conditions.

A vision is meant to move the organisation forward to where it would like to be. A precise goal is more credible than a vague dream. A vision should be realistic and attractive to all members of the organisation. As a condition, a vision should be more desirable in many important ways than the situation which currently exists. A specific definition of vision within the context of schools would be the school's aims. In the context of the Achievement for All programme the vision and aims should be notably achievement orientated.

Identifying shared values is the starting point when generating a vision for the school. This should be based on past and present values and might reflect what is good within the school. A genuinely good school with shared values and beliefs will be an effective school.

As stated, a vision must be shared, but it is the responsibility of leaders to ensure that vision 'happens'.

Vision aims for leaders and teachers

- To ensure that each child has a command of language and the ability to communicate effectively and confidently in reading, writing, speaking and listening.
- To develop a knowledge and understanding of basic mathematical facts and concepts and of how to use them.
- To encourage scientific curiosity and to organise observational studies, particularly in the local environment.
- To awaken children's awareness of their heritage, both local and national, and to give some understanding of their place in the world.
- To give an understanding of moral and ethical codes, religious beliefs and ideas, and of how to live with others.
- To teach skills and the appreciation of aesthetic qualities in the creative arts: art, craft, music and drama.
- To develop and maintain a healthy body by providing enjoyment in physical activities.
- To create a happy school environment.
- To help children learn that courtesy, good manners and consideration for others are very important qualities and to make each child a responsible member of the school community and also of the wider community.
- To encourage children to develop a habit of learning and to develop a lively enquiring mind and a cooperative attitude towards all the people who are working for the successful achievement of these aims.

In summary: inclusive leadership lessons learned

- To communicate vision to all stakeholders often (to make change occur).
- To distribute leadership/support staff to lead/take ownership to affect change.
- To provide high quality training to all staff.
- The senior leadership team must drive vision.
- To know the community/use initiative to build relationships with the community.
- To have a clear vision and expectations from the outset.
- To change processes/practices/structures/interventions if they are not working ('being able to say it was wrong and reviewing lessons learned – solution focused, open and honest').
- To give time to staff for communication of success and to learn lessons.
- The leaders must demonstrate a belief in new changes.
- To evaluate and celebrate successes.
- To involve staff in the development and implementation of Achievement for All.
- To use what you have learned for children with SEND to focus on wider groups of children within the school.
- To have courage and be a risk taker ('change and bend the rules to match your own context').

EFFECTIVE LEADERSHIP OF ACHIEVEMENT FOR ALL – CASE STUDIES

Vision

Vision becomes apparent in both informal and formal communications – staff meetings, conversations in corridors, meetings with parents and other agencies. Effective leaders are reflective thinkers, who are constantly evaluating, questioning and challenging current school practices and culture. They embed their belief that ALL children can achieve and make progress constantly. They are able to demonstrate:

- a core moral purpose
- consistent message and role-modelling

- knowledge and context of community
- accountability and responsibility
- self-awareness and ability to reflect
- risk-taking and innovation.

The following case studies demonstrate how two schools used Achievement for All to review their visions and values; the actions leaders have taken to develop and embed these; and some indication of the impact these have had on internal processes and outcomes for pupils.

Case study: Westwood School, Oldham

Context
As a pilot school for Achievement for All, Westwood saw this as an opportunity to impact positively on all children in their school, and not solely as a framework for improving the progress of pupils identified with SEND. Their belief was that Achievement for All would enable them to restate their vision and values and, importantly, to embed these in wider systems and practice.

Key challenges
Achievement for All was to be used to enable the school to take stock, reflect and evaluate the ownership of their vision and values, and plan for maximising their impact. This has been an ongoing process of reflection.

Approach
The leadership team recognised that Achievement for All was not an area that could be delegated; it had to be integral to the core values of the school if it was to succeed. They modelled the behaviours required in any school interactions, be they formal or informal.

Outcomes
Achievement for All has enabled the school to:

- reflect on, and evaluate its values and vision
- restate and communicate the vision
- act collectively to achieve the goals of the framework
- model behaviours required by leaders and teachers.

Case study: Lee Chapel Primary School, Essex

Context
The leadership team of the school was passionate about providing outstanding education that would improve the life chances of all their pupils identified with SEND. Viewing education as the key to improving life chances for their pupils, they were determined not to allow a ceiling to be put on a child's attainment because of their socio-economic background or SEND. So they did all in their power to remove any barriers, implementing the project quickly.

Key challenges
The leadership team recognised that sharing the vision of an Achievement for All action plan would be the major driver for a whole-school commitment to Achievement for All and, that the latter would be a challenge.

Approach
Through training days, the leadership team communicated the Achievement for All action plan to staff and their role within it. This approach was well received by all the staff. More in-depth conversations were arranged with staff regarding pupils' individual needs and every member of staff was encouraged to lead or support an Achievement for All activity.

Outcomes
The Achievement for All learning support assistants (LSAs) have taken on a 'team' identity, becoming a mutually supportive and collaborative group of professionals who are helping to drive the Achievement for All agenda in the school.

The LSAs have been empowered through CPD, coaching, observation and feedback, and the leadership's faith in their ability to make a difference. They have responded positively to the opportunities for skills development and for taking on more responsibilities as part of the school's team around a child.

There has been 100% take up of before-school, lunchtime and after-school interventions, activities and support.

Punctuality has improved 100% because the pupils are at breakfast club by 8a.m.

> **Review questions**
>
> - To what extent is the vision in your school shared by staff, governors, parents and pupils?
> - What strategies might you use to review and share that vision to ensure that all pupils achieve?
> - Why are school visions central to planning?
> - School organisational structure determines effective leadership. In your opinion, which organisational structural model might, in practice, be more effective? Why?
> - How would you define culture within the context of the school?
> - How would you ensure that the culture of your team reflected the culture of the school?
> - How would you ensure, as a leader (middle or senior), that you were continuing to make the school's vision 'happen'?

Commitment

Successful leaders reflect their commitment to their pupils through their behaviours as leaders and managers. They are relentless in securing the most appropriate provision. They commit to providing high quality resources and engage specialist staff where appropriate. They invest in ensuring effective strategies and systems are in place to track pupils' progress. They have a strategic view of what is needed to skill their workforce to improve inclusion, are committed to constant development of staff and successfully deploy appropriate staff to meet the needs of the individual. They ensure that time is committed in staff meetings and elsewhere to discussion and dialogue about improving provision for vulnerable pupils. They value the engagement with parents by committing time and resources to ensuring effective structured conversations can take place within and outside the school day. Above all, they secure the commitment of all staff and ensure that their commitment is underpinned by a sense of collective responsibility for the achievement of all pupils (NCSL, 2011).

The following case studies indicate how leaders secured the commitment of staff to the Achievement for All programme and also committed time and resources to ensure the success of activities like structured conversations with parents.

Case study: Bankwood Community Primary School, Sheffield

Context

Bankwood has 248 pupils on roll. Situated in the south west of Sheffield many of the pupils join the school from the nearby Children's Centre. The school has a higher than average proportion of children claiming FSM and serves an ethnically diverse community.

Key challenges

Bankwood School is on a journey of improvement and change. The leadership of the school recognised that to achieve their SEND goals it was crucial that they had a commitment to their values and vision.

Approach

Ownership and commitment were achieved by creating clear structures and systems to support a shared vision, and expectations were clarified with staff. Relevant professional development opportunities were identified and fed into performance management targets. This enabled the impact of staff training on classroom practice to be monitored. In addition, the leadership team undertook regular reviews with staff to discuss challenges and to celebrate success.

Structured conversations were introduced and initially modelled by members of the leadership team. This was crucial in monitoring understanding and buy-in to the vision.

Regular Achievement for All staff meetings were held to support staff and ensure commonality of process and progress. A termly review was held by the leadership team, which also provided an indicator of the effectiveness of the vision and the extent to which this was embedded throughout the school.

Outcomes

Achievement for All allowed the school to deliver the training required which allowed for the up-skilling of staff. It enabled the school to clarify expectations, share difficulties and celebrate successes as well as role-model effective practice and empower staff.

In addition, staff ownership of values and vision was developed, leading to more shared responsibility for outcomes.

Case study: Caedmon Primary School, Redcar and Cleveland

Context
Caedmon, is a smaller than average primary school, with 237 pupils on roll. The school serves the local community, where very few children have English as a second language. There is both a higher than average proportion of pupils with SEND and pupils claiming FSM.

Key challenge
A collective responsibility for SEND.

Approach
A status audit was completed by the whole school team in an attempt to enable collective responsibility towards improving inclusive practice within the school, and to create commitment to the overall school vision. Using the data from the audit, the leadership team created an implementation plan which identified roles and responsibilities, and gave a purpose which had clear objectives for each specific area of the school.

Results were then communicated to staff during a staff meeting. Ideas and opportunities were shared and further collaboration time was then given so that all staff felt ownership of the plan and, in time, would feel ownership of the outcomes.

Outcomes
One example of the impact achieved by this sort of commitment was more precise assessment and tracking, with more strategic interventions. This led to increased pupil progress of 1.7 average point score, enabled by tight, regular pupil progress meetings between members of the leadership team and class teachers.

Review questions
- How does the leadership in your school demonstrate a commitment to the vision and values held within the school?
- How do you ensure commitment to your vision is shared by all staff?

Collaboration

Successful provision to ensure that pupils identified with SEND progress and achieve wider outcomes requires a culture of collaboration – with and between staff, with parents and with other agencies. Effective collaboration relies on leaders in and across schools working together with a sense of collective responsibility for vulnerable learners and pupils identified with SEND. It also means that leaders are outward facing – they look beyond their own school, they show an appreciation and understanding that all schools are different, and that strengths and good practice can be shared. Effective leaders model shared working practices in school and between schools and phases of education. In the successful schools within the Achievement for All project, leadership is both a collaborative and distributed activity (NCSL, 2011).

The following examples illustrate how two schools have collaborated effectively with parents, the local family of schools and other agencies to improve outcomes for children and young people.

Case study: Huntcliffe Secondary, Redcar and Cleveland

Context
Effective collaboration maximises the impact of Achievement for All, particularly between school phases. The Huntcliffe School recognised that Achievement for All presented an opportunity for collaboration between their family cluster. This opportunity has now been realised and the school has become the collaboration 'hub' for its feeder schools.

Key challenges
The person leading Achievement for All for this family cluster did not have a background in SEND. The school wanted someone who displayed the leadership skills to drive Achievement for All through effectively and not someone who simply had SEND knowledge.

This resulted in leaders actively role-modelling positive collaboration, as they had to work closely with others to gain knowledge and expertise of effective practice in leading and teaching pupils identified with SEND.

Approach
By working collaboratively, the cluster agreed a strategy for embedding Achievement for All; identified and undertook collective CPD opportunities; developed a shared vision; worked to introduce a successful transition process for pupils between phases to ensure the continuity of vision, values and practice; and communicated jointly with parents.

Outcomes

A significant and positive outcome of this collaboration was that all of the schools moved away from traditional parents' evenings. Instead, they introduced structured whole-school conversations, which allowed parents to have more time with school staff and identify further achievement opportunities.

Impact

Achievement for All has enabled the schools to share vision, values and practices across phases and ensure continuity during transitions within and between school phases.

Case study: Lyng Hall Specialist Sports College and Community School, Coventry

Context

The headteacher has been instrumental in seeking out and negotiating partnership work with key external agencies including multi-disciplinary teams, Children and Adolescent Mental Health Services, social housing and social care.

Key challenges

It has taken a great deal of leadership time; however, the benefits have resulted in new working agreements with the Education Welfare Service and the Primary Care Trust.

Approach

External agency teams meet with a team from the school to talk about action to be taken with referrals, which the school brings along to discuss. Staff at the school will also negotiate on behalf of families, for example to bring forward medical appointments. Identified staff working collaboratively with parents over a period of time has been key to the success of Achievement for All. Once a supportive relationship has been developed with parents, they are very willing to accept help and advice, and to admit they also find it is a challenge to support their child.

Outcomes

The range of impressive outcomes of Achievement for All include the fact that persistent absence has reduced from 12% in 2008–2009 to 3.9% in 2009–2010.

The school is now established as a Citizen's Advice Bureau Outreach Centre, with advisers, a kiosk and an information centre for parents and the local community.

Review questions

- Using the Achievement for All framework, how could you improve collaboration and sharing of knowledge about learning styles and of pupils' ability to learn?
- How do you ensure that information about each pupil is shared – class to class, key stage to key stage, school to school?
- How are the transitions within school and between schools managed?

Communication

The successful leadership of SEND relies on effective communications at a range of levels – with pupils; with parents and carers; with staff in and between schools and other services/agencies. Successful leaders are good at engaging others. They nurture relationships with pupils and their parents or carers. They are good listeners and can demonstrate that they value the contribution of others. They invest time in communicating with parents.

Effective leaders articulate and communicate a vision which they encourage others to share and develop. They actively encourage formal and informal dialogue about strategies to improve the achievement for all pupils. They share information about pupils' attainment and progress and celebrate achievement. Through their communications they give value to wider outcomes as well as those reported in performance tables (NCSL, 2011).

Case study: Coundon Court, Coventry

Context
Communication, especially in large institutions can be challenging. Coundon Court, a large secondary school, realised this was something they would need to address at a very early stage in the Achievement for All pilot.

Key challenges
The headteacher realised the importance of communicating the purpose and objectives of the Achievement for All pilot. To reach the widest audience and achieve the greatest engagement, this communication was undertaken departmentally and all department leads were asked to undertake some action research. This aimed to demonstrate the impact of Achievement for All in each subject area but also increased the profile of SEND in the school.

Approach

Staff within the school wanted to create a culture of active listening and therefore quickly opened communication channels with pupils.

A group of 130 pupils were surveyed to gather their views on what would impact on their own learning and how they could be helped to achieve maximum progress. Using the results of the survey, an Achievement for All sports club was set up, as well as a cookery club, which led to students working towards a BTEC (Business and Technology Education Council) qualification. These clubs were filmed and outcomes fed back to all departments on an INSET day. This led to other departments investigating setting up their own clubs.

Outcomes

The school was able to demonstrate a commitment to listening to, and acting upon, feedback from students. It instigated new models for communication to reach the widest audience.

Case study: St Michael's Church of England Primary School, Camden

Context

An inner city primary school with 215 pupils, aged 3–11 years on roll. The school is very supportive of children with SEND. The school's latest Ofsted inspection (2010) rated its overall effectiveness as good.

Key challenge

To report to the governing body on improvements in leadership of Achievement for All.

Approach

The project leader produced a condensed guide to Achievement for All for staff and communicated this, enabling everyone to understand the project and where their role lay within the programme. Regular updates were produced, ensuring that staff had current knowledge of Achievement for All, including feedback from training.

A dedicated Achievement for All display board was created for staff, showing the leadership structure of Achievement for All, pupils' case files and targets, together with progress reviews, training feedback and a strand-by-strand section outlining the school's vision and aims to achieve Achievement for All targets. This visual board created opportunities for professional communication among staff which leaders within the school actively encouraged.

An Achievement for All 'thought wall' was put up in the staffroom and all staff were encouraged to share ideas. These were then discussed at senior management team meetings to ensure the staff's collective voice was heard and implemented in planning ways forward. They were pleased that the wall was instrumental in developing both formal and informal discussions and was a time-efficient method of sharing ideas and collaboration. Through the 'thought wall', all staff were engaged in thinking about improving behaviour in the playground, and some excellent ideas were contributed and implemented. This was a new, simple approach to address a whole-school concern which resulted in positive outcomes. The format can be used again and again.

Sharing the Achievement for All vision with the governing body was achieved by a presentation by the project leader. This was well received and she regularly updates them on progress.

Outcomes

The project leader developed more positive and effective relationships with parents through formal and informal conversations. Parents were invited into school to work alongside their children in a variety of ways and as a result parents readily accepted and supported Achievement for All. A coffee afternoon for all Achievement for All parents, with key teachers, the project leader and parent liaison coordinator acted as an open forum regarding inclusion, Achievement for All and their children. Attendance was very good and they were particularly pleased that parents used the forum to talk to one another and share experiences.

Impact

The school's Ofsted report, published in January 2010 noted that pupils identified with SEND make as much, if not more progress than other pupils.

Assessments show pupils identified with SEND, in most cases, are making a minimum of two points progress per term; of the pupils identified with SEND making progress, the majority have made four points progress.

The school's focus work on friendships and playground behaviour has shown playground incidents are less frequent and pupils are keen to win the half termly 'fabulous friends award'.

Review questions

- How effective are the systems for communication in your school?
- How do you encourage dialogue across the school about valuing and securing achievement for all pupils?

Conclusion

The National College review of characteristics of effective leaders found that, by adopting the Achievement for All framework, leaders:

- Have a clear core purpose and vision for educational practice in support of vulnerable learners, particularly those identified with SEND.
- Secure a commitment from everyone to the vision that ALL pupils can succeed.
- Work in collaboration and are accountable to improve outcomes for pupils identified with SEND.
- Are effective in communicating the message that ALL pupils, at whatever starting point, need or ability, will increase access and raise achievement within a culture of high aspiration.

Schools that have demonstrated **vision, commitment, communication** and **collaboration** have seen a significant impact on the progress of pupils identified with SEND by focusing on:

- assessment, tracking and intervention
- structured conversations and parental engagement
- improving wider outcomes.

Effective leadership is of vital importance to ensuring the positive impact of the Achievement for All.

After only one term of the introduction of the Achievement for All programme:

- Headteachers were happy with the support from their achievement coach.
- School champions liked working with the Achievement for All school handbook.
- Headteachers were happy with the value for money being provided to their school.
- School champions and headteachers were happy with the whole-school CPD training they had received.
- Headteachers have stated that working as an Achievement for All coach has been the best CPD they have received in their careers.

Summary

Leadership is fundamental to effective pedagogy. Teachers are classroom leaders, responsible for all pupils. Every lesson, every day, every week should impact on learning. This chapter has provided a rich description of the need for all leaders in education to demonstrate their ability to develop and embed Achievement for All through vision, commitment, collaboration and communication.

The impact of Achievement for All leadership

Achievement for All leadership impacts on:

- The status of SEND in each school.
- The development of clear strategies designed to support the progress of pupils identified with SEND.
- A distributive leadership and the development of other leaders within schools.
- Self-reflection and school self-evaluation.
- Improving pupils' learning, progress and wider outcomes.
- Parental engagement – listening to and taking account of the views of parents.
- Revisiting the vision and values of the school.
- Planning for sustainability and real change.
- Achievement, access and aspirations for all children.

References

Angelides, P., Antoniou, E. and Charalambous, C. (2010), 'Making sense of inclusion for leadership and schooling: a case study from Cyprus', *International Journal of Leadership in Education*, vol. 13, no. 3: 319–334.

Bass (1999), 'Two decades of research and development in transformational leadership', *European Journal of Work and Organisational Psychology*, vol. 8, no. 1: 9–32.

Beany, J. 2006, *Reaching out, reaching in*, Nottingham, NCSL.

Blandford, S. (2006), (2nd Ed.) *Middle Leadership in Schools: Harmonising Leadership and Learning*, Harlow: Pearson.

Blandford, S. (2010), *Achievement for All, Monitoring and Evaluation Report, Summer*, London: DfE.

Blandford, S. (2011), Leadership Report, no. 11, London, National Strategies.

Carter, K., Franey, T. and Payne, G. (2006), 'Reshaping the landscape: exploring the challenges of outward facing leadership with a system perspective' in Carter, K. and Sharpe, T. *School Leaders Leading the System: system leadership in perspective*, Nottingham: NCSL.

Carter, K. and Sharpe, T. (2006), *School Leaders Leading the System: system leadership in perspective*, Nottingham: NCSL.

Department for Children, Schools and Families (2009a), *Achievement for All: Guidance for Schools*, Nottingham: DCSF.

Department for Children, Schools and Families (2009b), *Achievement for All: Local Authority Prospectus*, Nottingham: DCSF.

Department for Children, Schools and Families (2010), *Breaking the link between special educational needs and low attainment*, Nottingham: DCSF.

Department for Education (1994), *Code of Practice on the Identification and Assessment of Special Educational Needs*, London: HMSO.

Fidler, B. (2002), *Strategic Management for School Development*, London: Paul Chapman Publishing.

Fullan, M. (2004), *System Thinkers in Action: Moving beyond the Standards Plateau*, London/Nottingham, DfES Innovation Unit/NCSL.

Fullan, M. (2007), *The New Meaning of Educational Change*, San Francisco, CA: Jossey-Bass.

Gibson, S. and Blandford, S. (2005), *Managing Special Educational Needs: A practical guide for primary and secondary schools*, London: Sage.

Gold, A., Evans, J., Earley, P., Halpin, D. and Collarbone, P. (2003), 'Principled Principals? Values-Driven Leadership: Evidence from Ten Case Studies of '"Outstanding" School Leaders', *Educational Management and Administration*, vol. 31, no. 2: 127–138.

Hopkins, D. (2007), *Every School a Great School*, Maidenhead: McGrawHill/Open University Press.

Kugelmass, J. and Ainscow, M. (2004), 'Leadership for inclusion: a comparison of international practices', *Journal of Research in Special Educational Needs*, vol. 4, no. 3: 133–141.

Kugelmass, J. W., 2003, *Inclusive Leadership: Leadership for inclusion*, New York, New York State University.

Lamb, B. (2009), *Lamb Inquiry: Special educational needs and parental confidence*, DCSF.

Manchester University (2010a), *Achievement for All National Evaluation, Interim Report*, May 2010, Manchester: Manchester University.

Manchester University (2010b), *Achievement for All National Evaluation, School Level Survey Report*, September 2010, Manchester: Manchester University.

National College for School Leadership (2009), *Achievement for All: Characteristics of effective inclusive leadership – a discussion document* Nottingham: NCSL.

National College for School Leadership (2011), Achievement for All: Leadership Matters, Nottingham: NCSL

O'Leary, D. and Craig, J. (2007), *System Leadership: lessons from the literature*, Nottingham: NCSL.

Sikes P., Lawson, H. and Parker, M. (2007), 'Voices on: teachers and teaching assistants talk about inclusion', *International Journal of Inclusive Education*, 11, 3, 355–370.

4 High quality teaching and learning

This chapter is in two sections:

1 Developing a framework for high quality teaching and learning in practice
2 Teaching and learning – case studies

Introduction – teaching and learning

Element two of the Achievement for All framework – high quality teaching and learning – supports schools to improve the attainment and progress of students with SEND, LAC, those claiming FSM and other vulnerable and disadvantaged learners. Its implementation is centred on the key areas of assessment, data tracking and target setting. In essence when there is a rigorous, high quality approach to these areas the attainment and progress of children and young learners is significantly improved. Evidence from the Achievement for All pilot highlighted its effectiveness in bridging the achievement gap for children with SEND. In English, 37% of children achieved or surpassed expected levels of progress for all pupils nationally; for maths this figure was 42%.

A key feature of the national evaluation of the Achievement for All pilot was the way the framework enabled schools to give teachers responsibility for the pupils in their classroom. In schools, this was led by senior leadership teams and supported through focused staff training. This re-alignment of accountability paths, which continues in the national roll-out of the programme, includes (adapted from Humphrey and Squires, 2011):

- Teachers taking a more active role in the assessment and monitoring of pupils with SEND.

- Structured conversations with parents (three per year for identified pupils between key teacher, parents and their child), enabling teachers to change their own and parents' expectations of pupils with SEND and recognise pupils potential.
- Changing teacher knowledge and understanding of pupils with SEND, resulting in a more personalised approach to teaching and learning within the classroom.
- Teachers seeing CPD and other training opportunities provided through Achievement for All and generally associated with structured conversations as very helpful and applying them in their daily interactions with other staff members and parents.
- In schools with increased pupil attainment and other improved outcomes, teachers being more frequently involved in reviewing individual pupil targets.
- Data-led discussions between the senior leadership team and class teachers, providing opportunities to identify pupils not making the expected progress and to finding appropriate interventions to help them.
- Teachers planning together for differentiation, allowing for greater focus on individual pupils.

Teacher effect on pupil attainment is well documented in the wider research literature (Barber and Mourshed, 2007; Chetty et al., 2011; Hanushek, 2011). Furthermore the Sutton Trust report, *Improving the impact of teachers on pupil achievement in the UK – interim findings* (Sept. 2011), highlighted the detrimental effect of poor performing teachers on pupils' attainment. For those from disadvantaged families, an under-performing teacher can leave the pupils as much as one year behind in their learning.

Evidence from the Achievement for All programme has shown that teacher development is implicit in the framework. The shift in teacher attitude to teaching and their development of more inclusive practices through the Achievement for All framework – as a result of a greater focus on identification of vulnerable learners, their needs, assessment and provision – supports and encourages raised teacher aspirations and expectations for all children. Through the structured conversations with parents, teachers become more aware of and develop a greater understanding of their pupils' needs and potential. This contributes to an increased sense of professional responsibility and ownership in the classroom; for example, the learning needs of pupils with SEND are no longer seen by teachers as the responsibility of the SENCO or TAs. The greater focus on the learning and development of children and young people with SEND and other vulnerable groups, along with training and guidance leads to more effective teacher approaches in pedagogical practice. In particular, practices become more inclusive, enabling teachers to more effectively meet the diverse needs of all pupils. In essence, through the Achievement for All framework with focused training, what was previously considered to be an extra practice becomes rooted in everyday practice.

The impact of the Achievement for All pilot was profound. Schools now have:

- More effective monitoring of Key Stage 4 progress against targets, allowing for more forensic, targeted interventions for students who needed them. The data is used in meetings between students and mentors to discuss how progress can be improved which has led to a positive impact on Key Stage 4 results. *(Rye College, Sussex)*
- A lead teacher for Achievement for All was appointed to support teachers in the use of Average Point Scores (APS) to help inform planning and next steps in the children's learning, with a primary focus on SEND children (not only for teachers within the school but also within the school cluster). The outcome was that good progress was made by all the Achievement for All children in Year 5 with 70% of pupils making at least two sub levels progress in reading and 50% of children making at least two sub levels progress in maths over an assessment period of two terms. *(Birkbeck Primary School, Bexley)*
- School leadership and rigorous assessment and tracking enabled Pupil Y to achieve significant accelerated academic progress. Pupil Y had been identified at School Action Plus for severe BESD. Along with violent and aggressive behaviours he also had frequent bouts of depression with threats of suicide. He was bullying and dominating towards his peers and had extremely low self-esteem. All previous interventions had been centred on BESD including for example, the use of a learning mentor, art therapist, social groups and behaviour management strategies, but without success. It was only tangible academic achievement that led to a significant increase in his self-confidence. Careful assessment and tracking using APP, one-to-one tuition and involving the pupil in setting his own Achievement for All targets were hugely effective strategies. From having level 1 in each subject at the end of Key Stage 1 and no evidence of progress in Year 5, he achieved a 4b in writing and a 5c in reading. *(Savile Park Primary School, Calderdale)*

DEVELOPING A FRAMEWORK FOR HIGH QUALITY TEACHING AND LEARNING IN PRACTICE

Element two of the Achievement for All framework is based on teachers, pupils and their parents knowing where the children are in their learning, where they are aiming to get and how to get them there. It is founded on collaborative working and active learning. For schools this means having good policies for marking and feedback, strong whole-school assessment systems in place and good monitoring and evaluation approaches to processes and practices. For teachers it means knowing the pupils and how they learn, having high aspirations for their learning, giving children a sense of ownership of learning, taking a more personalised approach to children's learning and keeping good records. For pupils it means being able to access the curriculum, raising their aspirations and increasing their achievements. Access will be closely connected to their own feelings of confidence: confidence in their competencies, high self-esteem and self-mastery skills. For parents it means knowing where their child is in their learning, knowing how to support them in their learning and having high aspirations for their learning and achievement. The following sections explore some of the key classroom practices related to assessing children, tracking progress and setting targets.

Assessment and target setting

Assessment is a cyclical process, which informs long-, medium- and short-term planning. It involves gathering evidence of pupils' learning, analysing and evalu- ating the evidence and allowing time to reflect on how to develop appropriate and aspirational learning targets, which include progression materials that inform appropriate target setting. Within the Achievement for All programme aspirational learning targets are set in conjunction with parents/carers. Teachers acknowledge that observing children first-hand informs teaching and provides opportunities to develop their learning. Developing a framework for common practice can margin- alise the element of subjectivity in all observation; it may take the format of a set of questions as in the box on the next page.

- What aspect of learning do I want to assess?
- What is the best way of collecting this data? (What type of observation?)
- What am I looking for? (Consider the National Curriculum and P scales.)
- What does it tell me about the child?
- What aspects do I need to consider to help this pupil develop/progress more independently?
- How much time do I need to give this child to develop this skill/progress in this area? (In the Achievement for All programme, you expect to see progress termly.)

Measuring the progress of pupils in special schools and those with complex needs in mainstream schools

Performance scales (P scales) are statutory when reporting attainment for pupils with SEND who are working below level 1 of the National Curriculum. They are recognised nationally, widely used and provide a standard means of measuring attainment of pupils with SEND. There are a number of assessment packages available on the market – for example, *PIVATS, B Squared*, with more currently being developed. They also use P scales, adapted to recognise further incremental attainment of pupils.

Knowledge and understanding of how data can be used to accurately assess pupil attainment and track progress is a positive move towards the development of a culture of high expectations. For learners working below level 1 of the National Curriculum their prior attainment at the beginning of each key stage is an important starting point for developing expectations and setting aspirational targets. The nature of a child's SEND should be taken into account when setting targets.

Across the school or clusters of schools it is important that effective procedures for moderation and standardisation are in place. In practice, this means all teachers and teaching staff employing the P scales in the same way. For example:

- Do all teachers have the same expectations for achieving a particular level?
- Do they know what this looks like in practice (what does the child have to do to achieve a particular level)?
- Are all teachers ensuring that children achieve a minimum number of indicators to be awarded that particular level (where there are a number of indicators for each level/sub level)?

Building children's confidence

Developing positive dispositions to learning is closely related to a child's level of confidence, which in turn can impact on motivation. Psychologists suggest that this is related to children's own theories about learning which produce certain recognised patterns of behaviour in approaching new learning challenges (Brooker and Broadbent, 2003, 51). Dweck (2000) refers to these patterns of behaviour as 'mastery-oriented' and 'helpless-oriented' behaviour. Children who display a mastery orientation towards a difficult task remain confident in attitude and approach, whereas those who display a helpless-orientation lose focus and concentration and adopt an attitude of failure. Effective formative assessment needs to be constructive. It should motivate children, moving them towards self-mastery. It is important to remember that children's confidence develops step by step and is fuelled by their successes: recall the adage 'success breeds success'. This is best achieved by focusing on the individual – their achievements and their continuing progress.

A sense of confidence is crucial for pupils navigating through school, giving them the strength to meet challenges and strive for what they want to achieve. The stigma attached to pupils with SEND, LAC, those on FSM and other vulnerable and disadvantaged learners can sometimes reduce child confidence and consequently decreases the likelihood of the child accessing the opportunities a school has to offer. The following provide examples of how Achievement for All schools have identified the issue and/or addressed it:

- It was noted that pupils with low confidence were less likely to attend extra-curricular activities both in and out of school. It was also suggested that low confidence led to less independent learning. *(Caludon Castle, Coventry)*
- Low self-esteem and confidence was linked in one school to difficulty in forming social relationships. Putting a target pupil in a position of responsibility gave him a sense of self-worth, increasing his confidence and his enthusiasm for learning. *(Saltburn Primary School, Redcar)*
- Structured conversations with a parent through telephone calls were found to help identify a pupil's lack of confidence, low self-esteem and difficulty in focusing and concentrating on literacy targets. The pupil's handwriting and presentation also improved. *(Saltburn Primary School, Redcar)*
- A parent group set up through Achievement for All have expressed enjoyment in understanding how their children learn and how they can help them. In this

small group, parents have grown in confidence and trust the staff enough to ask questions about levels, learning styles and so on, which they avoided in the usual school meetings. *(Redcar Community College, Redcar)*

- A range of interventions, developed and implemented through structured conversations, has provided success within reading, writing and maths, thus raising pupils' self-esteem as demonstrated by improved relationships, attitude to work (they will now have a go!) and general increased confidence. *(Beeston Fields Primary, Nottinghamshire)*

Involving pupils in self-assessment and discussion of their learning

Providing pupils with the opportunity to discuss their work provides a means of appropriately re-channelling their thinking. Black and Wiliam (1998:11) highlighted the benefits for pupils, in terms of improved knowledge and understanding, when they have the opportunity to discuss their work with teachers. Through Achievement for All, this takes place with teachers and other teaching staff in the classroom and during structured conversations with the parent, if the child is present. Often in the classroom, this will be questioning pupils about their work. To be of benefit, assessment needs to be given careful thought. The following has been adapted from Black and Wiliam (1998:11–12) and provides a good framework for considering how to use questioning effectively.

A framework for effective questioning

- Give pupils time to respond to questions (reflection time).
- Let pupils discuss their thinking in pairs before one of the 'pair' reports back (this tends to work better with older children).
- Give pupils a choice of answers and let them vote on the correct response.
- Good questions are hard to generate and practitioners should collaborate, and draw – critically – on outside sources, to collect such questions (it is good to write possible ways of both asking children questions and answering children's questions into short-term plans).

Good questioning is founded on the idea of teaching for independent learning. Practitioner questions should challenge pupils in their learning. They should provide opportunity for the pupils to start taking responsibility for their own learning, opening channels for thinking, creativity, problem-solving and decision making. Black and Wiliam (1998: 11) in their study of assessment highlighted the following:

> ...There are clearly recorded examples of such discussions (teacher–child) where teachers have, quite unconsciously, responded in ways that would inhibit the future learning of a pupil. What the examples have in common is that the practitioner is looking for a particular response and lacks the flexibility or the confidence to deal with the unexpected.

Motivational feedback (focusing on progress and success) is central to effective formative assessment and is closely linked to enabling pupils to be ready, willing and able to learn. The Assessment Reform Group (ARG) (2002) proposed Assessment for Learning approaches which 'protect the learners' autonomy, provide some choice and constructive feedback, and create opportunities'.

Marking and feedback

Constructive marking and feedback, if used appropriately by teachers, are powerful tools for enabling pupils to take ownership of their work and move towards self-motivated improvement. This has three core elements:

1 The pupil is fully aware of the learning objectives.
2 The pupil is made aware of the extent to which the learning objectives have been achieved.
3 The pupil knows how to go about achieving the shortfall in the learning objectives.

Feedback is most effective when pupils are enabled to act upon it. Shirley Clarke (1998: 70) suggests that effective feedback (at Key Stage 1 and beyond) needs:

- To be based on clear learning intentions.
- To take account of pupil self-evaluation.
- To highlight where success occurred and where improvement could take place.
- To be in a form accessible to the learner.

- To give strategies for improvement.
- Allocated time in which to take place or be read.
- Some focused improvement, based on the feedback to take place.

Involving pupils in planning their next steps

The last few years have witnessed a shift in classroom practice, particularly in the way pupils have become more involved in their own learning. There is the expectation that teachers, by making their pupils fully aware of the learning objectives and outcomes of a particular activity or lesson and involving them in planning their next steps, will enhance their learning. Clarke (2002) suggests balancing the curriculum to cover both the teaching of skills, concepts and knowledge and their application. Clarke says that sharing unit coverage throughout lessons and separating learning objectives from the context of learning will help pupils to be more aware of the goals on which they need to focus. Involving pupils in planning their learning helps them to take ownership of the work. For educators, this means guiding their pupils in their decision making; it is a time for guided choice, not free choice. There are also opportunities to involve children in 'what next?'

TEACHING AND LEARNING – CASE STUDIES

The following section considers, through case studies, how Achievement for All schools have effectively implemented and developed element two of the framework. They clearly show that, in practice, each element of the framework cannot be considered in isolation, but contributes to the whole programme.

Case study: Killisick Junior School, Nottingham

Context

Killisick is a small junior school with 160 pupils from a mixed catchment. The majority of children are white British with 10% of mainly white/black Caribbean mixed heritage. Around 40% are on FSM and the numbers of pupils with SEND is average – mostly they are pupils that find learning hard or who have behavioural, social and emotional difficulties.

Key challenges

Literacy had been a focus within the school for some time – children's reading levels and progress were 'Good', but the last full Ofsted inspection flagged up writing levels for attention and that now features in the SIP. Having thoroughly reviewed their literacy strategy, the school decided that it had become too formulaic and dry. They decided to introduce a more engaging, relevant and creative curriculum. They believed though that it was essential to have the flexibility to deliver an inclusive, whole-school programme with the ability to target appropriate groups, especially those identified with SEND.

The Achievement for All programme offered the school the opportunity to build on existing good practice and to enhance and give a higher profile to their SEND provision. The school joined the Achievement for All programme with other cluster schools to be able to share ideas, practice and impact.

Approach

Staff carried out a thorough analysis of their data across the school and scrutinised how well they knew each child. Having considered the results staff concluded that they needed to do more to understand their pupils, the reasons for their difficulties and to introduce appropriate solutions.

A key part of this for the senior leadership team was to ensure that they embodied the approach across the school, setting high expectations for all children regardless of their perceived ability. They took an open approach, sharing and discussing ideas with the whole team. They encouraged honesty and, while understanding that all teachers have been in the position of having a 'difficult' child in their class, they decided not to accept this view within their school community.

At their regular pupil progress meetings they realised that while they talked about the great progress many children were making there were some children that they never mentioned. They changed their approach, now the progress of every child is discussed and examined; they make sure that no child could become 'forgotten'.

Teaching and learning

The school introduced a creative curriculum making sure that children were totally immersed in a topic before being asked to write about it in literacy lessons. The main issue for them was that they felt children had insufficient knowledge or engagement with a subject and so by ensuring that a topic such as World War II was reflected through drama, art, history, music, PE and literacy they could offer multiple opportunities for children to learn about the subject in their different ways giving them enough stimulation to apply that to their writing.

Unusually for a Junior school they also chose to include role play areas in every classroom throughout the school to allow children to 'live' the part. In one particular lesson in Year 4, the classroom was blacked-out, the children dressed as evacuees complete with gas masks and the majority of the lesson was completed with the children under or behind their tables which the children had set up in 'rooms' within their new 'host family's house' for the morning.

In a Year 5 class during the Robin Hood topic, one boy who had been totally disengaged with literacy, had a 'breakthrough' point. The pupils were involved in constructing a giant hollow oak tree in one corner of the classroom. Following his involvement in a re-enactment of the story of Robin Hood this child sat down in the tree and wrote several lively and engaging pages of his experience. The transformation was stunning, he gained confidence and the difference was truly made.

Many of the changes the school made were practical. Reading sessions had been timetabled to take place after lunchtime and were proving challenging. These were moved throughout the school to take place at the beginning of the day, every day with a timetable of guided reading with the teacher, shared reading with a teaching assistant and independent reading.

Prior to engaging with Achievement for All, the school felt comprehension lessons lacked engagement. They now use topic-related texts as the basis for the 'response to text' activities, which form the final two sessions of their reading session timetable, again making them relevant to the child. They widened their range of reading materials including comic strip books, factual texts, online resources and films. They took part in the Premier League Reading Star programme.

They rarely take children out of class in the morning session for interventions –their belief is that all the children should take part in the class and have the benefit of that. However, all teachers and some teaching assistants have groups at assembly time, doing focussed working on writing or numeracy targets or addressing specific gaps they have identified in children's learning. There are also numerous intervention programmes running in the afternoons – including phonics lessons for around 50% of children. Spelling is an area they are working hard to improve – along with other basic skills including handwriting, for which the children have personalised targets.

Homework was another aspect of change. They found that giving out weekly writing homework meant that few pupils actually participated in it and often it was lacklustre. Instead they now give out homework every half term expecting the children to hand in four to five pieces over the course of the half term out of 16 optional projects offered, half linked to topics within the class and half to current topics of interest or the children's own interests. A piece linked to World War II asked pupils to design an air-raid shelter then to imagine what it must have been like to spend the night there and write about it.

Previously, only a handful of children in a class were completing the tasks – they now find that the majority participate. The school celebrates their successes and share their ideas, which encourages others to do their homework too. An unexpected outcome of this was the further inclusion of the wider family – parents and other family members participated in the work. One girl on the Achievement for All programme designed 'octo-girl' as part of her imaginary-worlds work – both her mother and her grandmother helped her to design and sew the toy.

The school also introduced 'teatime workshops' to help encourage parents to understand more about how literacy is taught in schools to further their support at home. They take place immediately after school and parents and their children are offered meals, the workshops include fun activities such as spelling and word games. Parents go into the classroom and teachers explain to them how teaching literacy happens; the school has written child and parent-friendly simple crib sheets to help them develop skills at home. Parents are carefully targeted, but it is hard to get them to attend. The school however, continues to focus on this area.

Above all the school has high expectations for all children – it expects them to apply learning independently, to behave well in class, to participate and progress.

In relation to data, during the course of Achievement for All, the school looked again at their data and identified that boys had particular issues with writing. They carried out pupil interviews to explore whether they were catering for their needs. The findings showed that boys wanted more film and online clips to illustrate materials; they particularly liked being in mixed groups with girls as they understood that the different approaches gave out more ideas; and they wanted topics to be relevant for them. The school made these changes and now ensures that all topics are engaging for both boys and girls such as including *Macbeth* within the Tudors module – the boys particularly like the battle scenes.

Outcomes

The key lessons for the school are related to expectations. They believe it is vitally important to have high expectations for all children and to have the flexibility and openness to identify and deliver that. For some of the changes it is early days, but over the past three years their writing levels have improved significantly. In 2011 of their 13 SEND boys, 11 achieved 13.5 points of progress and the remaining two achieved 12. Pupils identified with SEND are currently achieving level 5 in literacy. As of March 2012 Year 6 have made an average of 14 APS in reading with just three out of 41 children likely to fall below 12 APS by the time they take the SATs. In writing they have an average of 12.7 APS with around five of the children looking unlikely to make two full levels progress by the time they take the SATS – of these one has high levels of SEND and is working at P levels and has made good progress, and the remainder have joined Killisick since Year 3.

Instead of disaffection the school now has engagement and a motivated group of children who are willing to give things a go – and if, for whatever reason, they are not, the school has the strategies to help them achieve.

Review questions

- Consider the case study and outline the ways, from the outset to the final outcomes, that this school implemented and developed element two (high quality teaching and learning) of the Achievement for All framework.
- Consider your own school; are expectations for learning high enough? What could you do to improve them?

Case study: Hampstead School, Camden

Context

Hampstead School is an eight form entry inner-city secondary school serving an area to the north of the London Borough of Camden; many pupils from neighbouring boroughs also attend the school. The large majority of pupils are from minority ethnic backgrounds and around half speak EAL. Of the students, 25% are on the SEND register, and a significant number of pupils struggle to engage with learning. The school was designated as a specialist technology college in 1997 and the current headteacher joined the school in September 2006.

Approach

The SEND department identified improving behaviour for learning as a necessary development, to ensure pupils on the SEND register became effectively included in whole-class teaching and learning. Under the leadership of the headteacher and senior leadership team, the school linked up an existing health project being undertaken by the speech and language therapist together with a SEND specialist teacher to look at teaching and learning in the classroom. The school also undertook work to improve attendance, engage with parents, and reduce bullying.

Hampstead had already identified a need to improve learning in the classroom and had been working with a speech and language therapist. Through work with the Achievement for All coach they identified a programme to embed good listening and good behaviour for learning: Listen-EAR.

They looked at practice in the classroom and carried out an audit. This showed that many of the approaches used had become negative, for example, 'You need to listen better', and that pupils listened while they were being told off but would then switch off and continue with their disruptive or disengaged behaviour. A group of four teachers were then involved in developing and agreeing strategies and then working them through as a research project to develop a school plan.

Together they used the Listen-EAR techniques and toolkit and introduced this to the teachers. (The toolkit allows teachers to use a variety of techniques appropriate to a particular situation.) Essentially staff developed a set of classroom rules that applied to the teacher as well as the pupils. Many of these were common-sense approaches that teachers were already familiar with; but pulling these approaches together in one package allowed teachers to draw upon them constantly during lessons. Examples include following the practice that teacher and pupil look at each other while asking and responding to a question; counting up from zero for quiet rather than down from ten (which gives the teacher nowhere to go if zero is arrived at and peace has not been restored); using listening games to link to improvement in learning.

Part of the teacher learning was that, once the majority of the students were actively participating, it was much easier to identify those who were still struggling and take appropriate further interventions. For example, six boys were given six weeks of once-a-week lessons on improving listening and learning behaviour. Their behaviour improved which also meant less disruption in class for the other students. It also led then to identifying deeper student issues requiring level 3 interventions.

Outcomes

Training was given to staff in INSET days, led by these teachers presenting their successes to other staff. This was reinforced by the headteacher on the first day of term staff day, when he asked the Achievement for All champion to suggest two practical things teachers could do in the classroom that would make a difference.

In the second year of Achievement for All, Listen-EAR was extended to more teachers in Years 7 and 8 to ensure a critical mass of teaching expertise embeds the initiative. The Listen-EAR project enabled Achievement for All in Hampstead School to develop a lead approach to improving learning and attainment for target pupils. A number of vulnerable target pupils improved their progress in achieving two or more sub levels of attainment but crucially they developed improved attitudes towards learning and achievement. A second lesson study is now underway.

However, the initiative cannot work in isolation. Teachers and parents need to reinforce and support the techniques throughout the school and it needs to be integrated throughout the curriculum. Already Year 7 parents are informed of Listen-EAR and asked to help support good listening practice at home.

Impact

Figures show that 65% of pupils believed their listening and learning had improved during the course of the project. As a consequence of their understanding of the listening rules, pupils were able also to identify the most effective strategies used by staff. This information has been fed back to staff and is now being used to inform the development of the school's behaviour policy.

Initiatives around improved listening skills have been rolled out across the whole school. Quieter students feel more able to participate and teachers feel they have a lot of positive strategies they can use with clear reward and sanction links.

A teacher states: 'I've been a teacher for 20 years, but I was presented with a very challenging group of students in Year 7. The ability to use the Achievement for All and Listen-EAR techniques and strategies is what made the difference to me and to them.'

Review questions

- Consider the case study and outline the ways the school implemented the programme.
- Why do you think it was successful?

Summary

High quality teaching and learning, implemented and developed in schools through the integrated Achievement for All model provides an effective means of improving children's progress and raising their attainment. Through focused training, teaching staff develop their pedagogical skills and professional practice. Implemented at the school level and directing attention to aspects of teaching and teacher quality, the programme enables teacher development, without focusing on individual teacher performance.

References

Assessment Reform Group (ARG) (2002), *Assessment for Learning: 10 Principles*: ARG.

Barber, M. and Mourshead, M. (2007) How the world's Best Performing School Systems come Out on top: McKinsey.

Black, P. and Wiliam, D. (1998), *Inside the Black Box: Raising standards through classroom assessment*, London: NfER Nelson.

Blandford, S., Tavlos, L., Williams, K., Crowhurst, M. and Knowles, C. (2012), *Achievement for All Anthology, Pilot 2009–2011*, Nottingham: DfE.

Brooker, L. and Broadbent, L. 2003, Personal, social and emotional development: The child makes meaning in a social world. In *Learning in the early years: A guide for teachers of children 3–7*, (ed.) J. Riley, 9–61, London: Paul Chapman.

Chetty, R., Friedman, J. and Rockoff, J. (2011), 'The long-term impacts of teachers: teacher value-added and student outcomes in adulthood', *National Bureau of Economic Research*, Working Paper no. 17699.

Clarke, S. (1998), *Targeting Assessment in the Primary Classroom*, Abingdon, Oxon: Hodder and Stoughton.

Clarke, S. (2002), *Formative Assessment in Action: weaving the elements together*, Abingdon, Oxon: Hodder Murray.

Dweck, C. 2000, *Self-theories: Their role in motivation, personality and development*, Hove, East Sussex: Psychology Press.

Hanushek, E.A. (2011), 'The economic value of higher teacher quality', *Economics of Education Review*, vol. 30: 466–479.

Humphrey, N. and Squires, G. (2011), *Achievement for All: National Evaluation Final Report*, Nottingham: DfE.

Sutton Trust (2011), *Improving the impact of teachers on pupil achievement in the UK – interim findings*, London: (Sept. 2011).

5 Parental engagement

This chapter is presented in two sections:

1 Parental engagement – what can we learn from the evidence base?
2 Structured conversations – case studies

Introduction – the importance of engaging parents

In 2008, Brian Lamb was commissioned by the then Secretary of State for Children, Schools and Families to make recommendations on how to increase the attainment and achievement of young people with SEND.

The recommendations built on the *Lamb Inquiry into Parental Confidence in Special Education Needs* (2009) and stated that changes should be made to how SEND is identified in young people, that schools should be more accountable for the progress of low-achieving learners, and that schools should be supported in setting high aspirations for all, focusing on attainment, engaging parents and developing wider outcomes. These recommendations became the foundations of the Achievement for All programme.

Engaging with parents is the third element of the Achievement for All framework and has been central to the success of the programme in raising the aspirations and achievement of children with SEND, those claiming FSM and LAC. Evidence from the national Achievement for All evaluation of the pilot (Humphrey and Squires, 2011) suggested that the particular open dialogue approach – developed through a series of three structured conversations between key teachers and parents and, if appropriate, their children – provided a platform from which parents could effectively engage in the learning process. Based on the idea of giving parents and carers of children with SEND, or other vulnerable learners, the opportunity to discuss their aspirations for their children, Achievement for All has provided schools with a framework to do this more effectively.

By considering the evidence base for parental engagement leading to improved outcomes for children, this chapter will explore the principles underpinning structured conversations and look at practical examples of where Achievement for All schools have effectively engaged parents to increase their children's aspirations, access and achievement.

PARENTAL ENGAGEMENT – WHAT CAN WE LEARN FROM THE EVIDENCE BASE?

The association between parental support of children's education and their academic achievement is widely supported by the research literature (Desforges and Abouchaar, 2003; O'Brien and Shemilt, 2003; Harris and Goodall, 2007; Goodall et al., 2011; Gorard et al., 2012 and OECD, 2011). This is promoted in UK government policy and reflected in wider government documentation (DfES, 2004). Examples of parents supporting children's learning include: at home, through homework, talking to them, reading to them; at school, volunteering in school, attending parents' evenings and through school–home partnerships. Here traditionally parents engage in their children's learning, for example attending meetings with teachers to discuss their children and aspirations for them, setting targets, and parent–child learning together programmes.

A review of the literature highlights the complexity in either clearly defining parental support or in 'distilling' the effect from other variables. Parameters are frequently set by the researchers with the result that measurement of parental involvement and parental engagement is subjective; this is generally explored through parental support within the context of either parental involvement or parental engagement. Frequently, both terms are used interchangeably, where neither term is clearly defined. Gorard et al. (2012) in their review of related literature cite 'parent as teacher and parent–school alignment' as the two principal mechanisms through which parental involvement impacts on children's attainment. Harris and Goodall (2007: 38–68) on the other hand, highlight the nature of parental engagement, which 'is not about engaging with the school, but with the learning of the child' and where 'engagement implies that parents are an essential part of the learning process, an extended part of the pedagogic process'.

The holistic view of parental engagement provided by Harris and Goodall (2007) is reflected in the Achievement for All model implemented across schools in England.

During the course of the national roll-out of Achievement for All, there have also been examples of effective 'parent–school alignment' and 'parent as teacher' which have had a big impact on children's attainment; Gorard et al. (2012) would classify this as 'parental involvement'.

Element three of the Achievement for All framework – parental engagement through structured conversations– has been developed from an evidence base of what works for children in the key areas of access, aspiration and achievement. Further enhancement, refined through the pilot, has resulted in the development of an effective integrated model of parental engagement in children's learning. The following section considers key research in this area, some of which informed the development of the Achievement for All model.

Parental involvement

Peters et al. (2007) in their survey of parental involvement in children's education found that a third of parents help their children with homework. The survey included a sample of 5,032 parents and carers of children aged five to 16 attending maintained schools in England; data was collected via telephone interview. Findings tended to indicate that parents are now more involved in activities at home with their children than previously. Figures reveal that 83% of parents do projects with their children (2004: 79%); 81% make things with their children (2004: 74%); 80% play sport (2004: 71%); and 79% are involved in their children's reading (2004: 70%).

Catsambis (2001) explored the link between parental involvement practices and the educational outcomes of high-school seniors. Data was drawn from the National Educational Longitudinal Study (NELS: 88), a study exploring student progress from eighth grade through to work. Using studies from 1988 (base-year) and 1992 (second follow-up year), the only years parental data was included, Catsambis employed data from 13,580 parents and their children. Using factor analysis to identify parent indices in line with Epstein (1992, 1995) parameters for parental involvement, different indices were employed for eighth and twelfth grade parental involvement. Various socio-economic factors and other demographic characteristics were controlled.

Findings showed that parental involvement in the eighth grade has little or no impact on student achievement growth during high school. Parental expectations and encouragement for college have the highest positive association with student achievement. Findings further showed that a very strong link in the context of parental involvement is that between parental monitoring of coursework and student achievement. Findings showed that when parents monitored their children's coursework in high school, students achieved more credits in English and science.

Employing data from the National Child Development Study (NCDS), a longitudinal study of children born in the UK in one week in March 1958, Hango (2007) explored mother and father involvement of children's academic outcomes. The original data in the NCDS included 17,000 mothers (98% of births that week) with follow-up interviews at age seven, 11, 16, 23 and 42. Employing a two-phased approach, Hango considered the link between children from disadvantaged families and education at the age of seven and father and mother involvement at age 11. The second phase considered the same variables at 16 years. In the final instance, with various restrictions imposed on the data by the researcher, the sample included data from 3,072 participants in phase one and 2,658 in phase two.

In measuring parental involvement at the age of 11, Hango considered both teacher assessment of parental involvement and parent perception of their involvement; the latter focused on the frequency of child-parent outings. For phase two he considered parental involvement in the context of how well the child and parent 'got on' (child perception). Overall findings showed that parental involvement of both the mother and the father was greater for parents with higher qualifications. In addition, although outings with the mother and the father's interest in education had a positive impact on future qualifications, the father's social class, living in an owner-occupied house, the child's gender, behaviour and reading ability were the most relevant indicators of later achievement (as measured by future qualifications).

In the Netherlands, Kloosterman et al. (2011) explored parental reading socialisation and school involvement on children's attainment and progress during primary school. Drawing data from the Dutch Cohort Study Primary Education (PRIMA), a biennial study examining the cognitive ability and social skills of Dutch primary school children, the researchers considered data for 11,916 second-grade pupils (five to six years old) in 587 primary schools. Data provided details on family social status and pupil language and maths performance in grades 2, 4, 6, and 8 for school years 1996/97, 1998/99, 2000/2001 and 2002/2003. Attrition was approximately 20% at each measurement point, with greatest attrition among disadvantaged children.

Researchers measured parental involvement through four indicators: frequency with which parents spoke to their child about school-related issues (parental data), frequency parents attended school meetings (parental data), the extent to which parents had good contact with the school (teacher data) and the extent they were actively involved with the school (teacher data). Findings showed that both parental school involvement and parental reading socialisation have an impact on children's language development; the impact on maths achievement was not strong. Findings further showed that over the course of primary schooling, the effect of early parental reading instruction had a positive impact on children's language performance.

De Fraja et al. (2010) explored the impact of parental, teacher and pupil effort on children's achievement. Employing data from the British National Child Development Study (NCDS), the researchers measured children's effort through their attitude (for example, what they think of school), parental effort through their interest in their children's education (for example, frequency of reading to the children and attendance at school meetings) and teacher effort through their perception of the school's involvement with the parent (for example, does the school initiate contact or involvement with parents). Findings showed a multiplier effect in the parent–child effort; that is, the researchers found that parental effort 'induces' children to make more effort, which pleases the parent, and so on. Interestingly, their findings further showed that schools have a positive response to children's effort, but not to parents.

Flouri and Buchanan (2004) explored the role of the father's and mother's involvement in their child's later attainment. The roles were considered independently. They drew data from the National Child Development Study on 3,303 individuals, which had details of the father's involvement at the age of seven, the mother's involvement at the age of seven, and qualifications on leaving school by the age of 20. Measures of involvement included reading to the child, going on outings with the child, taking an interest in the child's education and the father managing the child. Findings suggested that father and mother involvement at the age of seven predicted educational attainment by age 20. In highlighting weaknesses in the data the researchers refer to the greater attrition of disadvantaged children over the years.

Flouri (2006) considered, among other issues, the impact of the mother's and father's interest in their child's education on educational attainment aged 26. Controlling for various socio-economic factors, the findings showed that the mother's interest was closely associated with educational attainment in both men and women. Findings further showed that for women, the father's interest in education positively impacted on their later educational attainment; for men, the father's interest indirectly impacted, by increasing the mother's involvement. The researcher concluded that parental interest had an impact on later educational attainment, but this relationship was stronger for women than men.

In America, Topor et al. (2010) explored how parental involvement increases pupil academic performance. Employing a sample of 158 children at seven years old, their mothers and their teachers, the researchers found a statistically significant association between parental involvement and a child's achievement; this was found to be over and above that of the child's intelligence. Participants were from three different groups, participating in a larger longitudinal study and included a cross-section of children (in social and ethnic background). Various standard measuring instruments were used to assess parental involvement, the relationship between student and teacher, the children's cognitive and physical competence along with peer and mother social acceptance and the children's academic performance.

In considering the mechanism for parental involvement on children's achievement, the findings showed that parental involvement positively impacts on children's perception of their cognitive competence and on the student–teacher relationship. The researchers concluded that these factors contributed to increased academic performance in the children, where the former led to increased achievement test scores for the children, while better student–teacher relationships resulted in higher academic performance in the classroom.

Parental engagement

Evangelou et al. (2005) provided an example of a parent support programme in their evaluation of the Peers Early Education Project (PEEP). The project was estab-lished in 1995 as an early intervention programme focused on supporting parents as educators of their children. Involving a sample of 300 children aged from birth to five years old and an equal number in a control, participants were identified from four housing estates in Oxford. As an early intervention programme, it aimed to increase children's attainment, particularly in literacy, by supporting parents in reading to and with their children, talking to them and also included play and singing activities. Findings highlighted the benefits to children's literacy development aged five, where it was particularly beneficial for children at risk of low achievement.

Nutbrown et al. (2005) considered the Raising Early Achievement in Literacy (REAL) project, a pre-school literacy intervention, which was established in Sheffield in 1995. Aimed at three to four year olds and their families, the project included 16 children in four children's centres; a control group was established. Children were identified, from among those who it was considered would benefit from the project; their families were invited to participate. The approach of the intervention involved a number of home visits to families and attendance at events.

Findings showed that children in the intervention group had higher levels of achievement in language and literacy compared to those in the control group. For children of mothers with no qualifications, the benefits extended to the age of seven.

Sylva et al. (2008) explored the impact of the Supporting Parents on Kids Education in School (SPOKES), a parent training programme set up in eight schools in disadvantaged areas of London. The programme aimed to improve children's behaviour and literacy and was implemented over the 2001–2002 academic year; parents were given training in both areas. Taking part in the programme were 104 children aged four to six years, with participants being randomly assigned to a control or intervention group. Findings showed that children in the intervention group showed gains in both reading and writing. In relation to reading progress, the gain was equivalent to six months.

Erion (2006) provided a meta-analysis of research relating to parents tutoring their children. He considered studies up to the end of 2004, all of which focused on improvement in reading, maths or spelling; only five related to maths. Although Erion highlighted the relatively small body of literature reviewed and various short-comings in some of the evidence presented in the research, he concluded that parent tutoring leads to positive outcomes for their children.

Nye et al. (2006), in their systematic review of research related to parental involvement and academic performance of elementary school children in the USA, employed stringent criteria in the identification of research for inclusion in the study. Defining parental involvement as 'the active engagement of a parent with their child outside of the school day in an activity which centres on enhancing academic performance', they conclude that parental involvement has a 'significant' impact on children's academic performance.

It is clear that the research within this chapter provides evidence for improved academic outcomes for children when their parents become engaged and involved in the process.

In practical terms, the evidence suggests quite simple practices: parents showing an interest in their children's learning (De Fraja et al., 2010), which has a multiplier effect; parents having high expectations and encouraging their children (Catsambis, 2001) and parents reading to and talking with their children (Evangelou et al., 2005). The evidence also highlights the relevance of early parental interaction (Nutbrown et al., 2005), the long-term impact on future qualifications and the better involvement of parents with higher qualifications (Hango, 2007). Topor et al. (2010) in the USA give consideration to the mechanism through which parental involvement and engagement works in children – firstly by increasing the children's confidence in their own competencies and secondly by improving the child–teacher relationship. As Peters et al. (2007) survey shows, parents are generally more involved in activities with their children today than they were in past years. However, some parents do not realise they have a place in their children's learning; others do not know how to get involved.

The Achievement for All programme has been particularly successful in engaging parents from all groups in their children's learning. The following section considers case studies of how this has been achieved in schools through structured conversations, a central aspect of parental engagement.

STRUCTURED CONVERSATIONS – CASE STUDIES

Parental engagement is at the centre of the Achievement for All framework. Structured conversations between parents or carers and teachers have improved parental engagement with the schools and their involvement in their child's learning and achievement.

This element of the programme has had a significant impact on pupils and parents, changing families' lives and enhancing life chances.

Parental engagement has a very distinct and wide-reaching effect on pupil aspirations. Parents with low aspirations often pass this on to children. Furthermore, parents who do not understand the education system of which their child is a part may struggle to communicate aspirations to their children. Without modelling an aspirational outlook, it can be difficult for children to have their own.

The headteacher at Harbour School, Sussex supports a neighbouring school where she has shared her positive experience of engaging in Achievement for All.

> *The Achievement for All programme resonated with us all at Harbour, with its high focus on engaging parents and enlisting them as real partners – setting shared goals for the children and working together towards these. Having participated in a structured conversation, and set shared goals, we wanted to stay in touch with parents to track children's progress towards these goals together regularly. We knew it would be difficult to do this by face-to-face meetings alone, and decided to use the technology available to us as well. We decided to use the children's e-portfolio space...*

Founded on open channels of communication with parents, structured conversations enable schools to focus on three things:

1 How best to contact parents and, in some cases, remove communication barriers.
2 How to align the structured conversations to target setting.
3 How to engage children better in their learning.

Case study: Chosen Hill, Gloucestershire

Context

For Chosen Hill in Gloucestershire, an 11–18 academy converter, the introduction of Achievement for All coincided with a new pastoral system. A learning leader now heads up a team of eight tutors in each year group, whose role also includes academic monitoring.

Key challenges

The school lead and deputy head decided to focus on the role of the tutor in structured conversations, in spite of certain reservations. (Would they have enough knowledge in SEND? With the school already engaged in major change, would this be a step too far?) On the other hand, the SIP had already highlighted the need to develop more inclusive practices and focus all roles in the school on learning, so the decision was made.

Approach

When it came to implementing structured conversations, the key teachers (or tutors) were provided with in-school training. In addition, the inclusion manager developed a SEND information pack for each key teacher. The school then held an information evening for parents of SEND students, after which the school administrator arranged appointments by telephone for the first structured conversations.

Outcomes

The informal feedback from parents was very good. Everyone appreciated the opportunity to talk about their child's issues in a relaxed setting. In fact one parent later wrote to us, prior to transferring to another school at the end of Year 7, telling us that they hoped to find another Achievement for All school; they expressed strong appreciation for the provision offered.

The inclusion manager, reflecting on the first year of Achievement for All in relation to Year 7, says, 'I have never experienced such a close engagement in matters of SEND by tutors.' She believes that this is particularly significant and shows a positive inclusive shift for the school.

Impact

Considering other ways it had impacted on the school, the deputy headteacher said the following:

Key teachers are more confident when liaising with subject staff over issues relating to children's performance as their knowledge, understanding and sensitivity to this group of students has improved. This has undoubtedly benefited their teaching and learning within their own specialist areas.

In relation to students, because they are regularly involved in the learning process with parents and teachers, the structured conversations have helped them develop self-esteem. Talking together has helped some students alleviate stress and frustration; developing targets together has led to a shared language that all partners can relate to, and this in itself has supported students in accessing the curriculum and giving them an understanding of what 'progress' looks like. Students are beginning to see that learning is a journey in which everyone can take part. Their aspirations have increased through better identification of the small steps needed to achieve their longer term goals.

(Comments within the case study have been adapted from an interview with the deputy headteacher and project lead, along with the inclusion manager.)

Review questions

- Consider all the ways you 'engage 'parents in their children's learning.
- How could you engage parents more effectively in their children's learning?

For parents, structured conversations provide a forum to engage with their child's school, speak about their child's interests and learning, and their aspirations for their child. It is an opportunity to enhance and further develop their aspirations and to communicate this to their child. For schools, structured conversations provide time to listen to parents, talk to parents about their children's learning and reflect upon ways to transfer this to the classroom.

The effectiveness of this approach is reflected in the comments made by parents of children with SEND who participated in the pilot:

I feel listened to and really valued in the structured conversations. (Year 5 parent)

I know exactly what type of support my son is receiving and what his targets are so that I can help him more too. (Year 5 parent)

My son is now more confident, he interacts better, he is learning more and he feels better about himself. He used to really struggle and was so clingy with me. (Year 1 parent)

Case study: Badger Hill Primary School, Redcar and Cleveland

Context
Badger Hill is a rural primary school, situated in Redcar and Cleveland. It has 240 pupils on roll between the ages of 3–11 years. Its most recent Ofsted report was good.

Key challenges
A key aim in joining Achievement for All was to improve the attainments of low-achieving pupils. The headteacher wanted to close the achievement gap and enable every SEND pupil to reach their potential. To ensure each child had the best opportunity, TAs were redeployed, being moved from main lessons to focus on pupils identified with SEND. Two pupils in particular were considered. The headteacher saw parental engagement as being central to school improvement, and structured conversations a key factor in increasing achievement and aspirations. Parental engagement was already a focus in the School Development Plan. In starting structured conversations with one year group, the headteacher aimed, over the short term, to hold structured conversations with the parents of every child. The headteacher underlined the success of early conversations with parents who attended: 'Parents love that it is relaxed and they were contributing and they like this'.

In relation to parental engagement, there were both internal and external challenges in implementing this element of the programme. These involved ensuring that staff would both 'buy into' and give the necessary time to structured conversations and that disengaged parents would engage with it; two out of three parents did not turn up for the first structured conversation.

Approach
Initially, eight children in Year 3 were identified to participate in Achievement for All. Seven were under achieving and one, although not underachieving, had Autism Spectrum Disorder (ASD). However, very quickly the school champion decided to focus Achievement for All on all Year 3 children. The headteacher invited the most enthusiastic member of staff to lead Achievement for All within the year group (Year 3). Staff meetings were arranged and the basic principles outlined.

Parents' views of structured conversations were very important to the school and, following their initial feedback, language which was alien to parents' day-to-day language was removed. Following the modification, feedback sheets were given to parents at the outset of the structured conversations for them to note their opinions, their child's opinions and that of their teacher. The sheet gives a summary of the child's progress against set targets.

Outcomes

Structured conversations were central to the success of the programme. It was noticed that parents were more open about coming into the school and about coming in to discuss their relationship with their child. Additionally, the school increased the support it provides to parents under the umbrella of 'parenting skills'. The following shows one practical way this was done:

> *Pupil S never went to bed before 10 in the evening. Her mother could not cope with her. One day, her mother aired her concerns to her teacher. Pupil S was always tired and lacked concentration. The school's response was immediate. The school arranged for Pupil S to have a diary, where she was asked to keep a record of everything she did at home, at school and to record the time she went to bed. She brought this to school daily. Pupil S is now more alert at school and has better concentration; she has improved in four benchmarks.*

Review questions

In the case study, consider how the school involved parents.

- How did the school support parents to engage with their children's learning?
- How would you have involved and supported parents? (Consider this from your school's point of view.)
- How would you involve 'hard to reach' parents?

Case study: Brightside Infant and Nursery School, Sheffield

Context

Brightside Infant and Nursery is an inner-city school where 35% of the pupils have EAL; language barriers are the greatest challenge for the school. Its most recent Ofsted rating was outstanding.

Approach

Initially six pupils with SEND were identified in Year 2 to participate in the Achievement for All programme. Pupils included a girl in foster care and three EAL (Roma Slovakia) children. Training for all staff in structured conversations was year group specific; the Achievement for All pro forma was modified to suit the local situation.

The following case study with one child in the Achievement for All cohort provides an example of how the structured conversations work in practice.

First structured conversation
At the outset Pupil J's mother was disengaged from her child's learning. During the first structured conversation, Pupil J's class teacher and the TA met with his mother. Initially, to help secure home–school continuity, they identified which parent would work with Pupil J at home. The staff listened to the mother's concerns about her child and his learning. Together they came up with targets. She agreed to be the parent at home responsible for supporting his learning. They agreed that, at home, Pupil J's mother would focus on his fine-motor skills. Strategies for doing this were discussed; those used at both home and school were similar. After the first structured conversation the mother was given a copy of the write-up.

Second structured conversation
At the second meeting, Pupil J's mother spoke of happiness at seeing the improvements in her child's learning and development. His class teacher, TA and mother discussed his previous targets; his goals were written at the top of the page, to be seen clearly. Together they considered other ideas for working at home. The teacher suggested that one effective activity would be that of playing with dough and cutters.

Outcome

Structured conversations are not carried out in isolation and parental engagement is further supported by the school. The following is an outline of other ways Brightside Infant and Nursery School supported structured conversations to improve children's outcomes.

- Individual targets for children were put up in the resource room.
- TAs working with children were given their targets.
- Targets were built into planning.
- Parent workshops took place every half-term, for example, a workshop on phonics. (A high proportion of Achievement for All targets are related to reading and the SENCO noticed that parents did not have the knowledge to support their children at home.)
- Necessary resources were made available for parents.
- Targets were reiterated, and their importance for parents were explained.
- A number of lunchtime clubs for children were started, for example art club.

Review questions

- Outline the content and approach of structured conversations.
- What other ways would you have used to support parents in engaging with their children's learning?
- How do structured conversations improve children's outcomes?
- How can teachers transfer the outcomes from a structured conversation into teaching and learning within the classroom?

Case study: Alexandra Park Primary Junior School, Oldham

Context

Alexandra Park is a primary junior school, educating children from 7–11 years (Year 3 to Year 6). Situated in an inner city, with 290 pupils on roll, 100% of the children are EAL. Parental engagement had been a strong focus within the school, but Achievement for All provided the framework to develop this further in a more effective way. Analysis had highlighted the poor engagement of the parents of pupils with SEND.

Approach

Initially the school focused on the lowest achieving 20% in Year 3 and Year 5, but involved the whole-school in structured conversations and wider outcomes; Achievement for All became part of the School Development Plan. Teachers were trained in structured conversations with parents. Parental attendance at the meetings was tracked (currently 92% attendance) and non-attending parents were rigorously followed up. Early impacts were very positive. The Achievement Coach commented on the improved relationships and contacts with parents and the continuity between home and school for the children.

Impact

The following considers the impact of the structured conversations on parental engagement through the voice of the teachers involved:

Before Achievement for All
Previous to this year I felt I was rushed as all the parents came at once to look at their child's books and collect reports. I did not feel I could speak in full to each parent properly on a one-to-one basis.
Initial parent meetings were quite focused and targets etc. were discussed in detail, but there was no effective follow up on a regular basis.
It was difficult to talk to parents, most just collected reports and didn't stay.
It used to be mainly me talking to the parents telling them what subjects their child is good at and what levels they are on.

After Achievement for All training
The interaction has improved because we get time to speak to each parent and child individually rather than in a classroom full of parents...We are able to focus attention on one person at a time.
We have more focused discussions around all areas of the child's progress, attitude and behaviour. Parents were involved and responsible.
The interaction was much better; the structure has really helped focus the meeting...It has made me more aware of how they [parents] can help their child at home.
I gave the parents more opportunity to talk and direct the conversation. They told me of any issues they had/have at home. Parents are happy to help children at home.

Impact on learners in the classroom
The children seem to enjoy their parents hearing about the progress they are making. They like to know what to do next to reach levels.
Inclusion of the child is integral to the process. Each child is clear about their targets and what they need to do to achieve them.
Children are aware of what to do at home and are supported in class. I am receiving a lot more homework which is completed to a good standard.

Review questions

- Considering the case study above and the comments made (before and after), what were the key factors which contributed to improved parental engagement?
- What strategies do you use to engage all parents in your school?
- Why do you think structured conversations have been so effective in engaging parents in their children's learning?

Further insights

- Through structured conversations, Achievement for All provides opportunities for pupils and parents to discuss aspirational targets and actions. This has given the meetings purpose and parents have seen that the school is interested in their child's achievement, thus altering their mind-set about the school's aims. (*Beeston Fields Primary, Nottinghamshire*)
- Dialogue also helps foster an open and trusting relationship, which broadens parents' outlook. With parents being honest about what's happening at home and helping teachers understand pupils better, more focused targets can be set. (*Carlton Primary School, Camden*)

- Structured conversations with a parent through telephone calls were found to help identify a pupil's lack of confidence, low self-esteem and difficulty in focusing and concentrating on literacy targets. The pupil's handwriting and presentation also improved. (*Saltburn Primary School, Redcar*)
- Parental aspirations have been raised through Achievement for All by involving parents in decision-making processes, giving them the opportunity to express their views and aspirations for their child. (*Orchard Primary School, Sidcup*)

Summary

The Achievement for All programme is continuing to develop parental engagement through focused activities aligned to pupil progress. Our experience to date has been that all parents or carers, irrespective of their personal circumstances, want the best for their child. This chapter has provided qualitative evidence of the impact of a shared approach to supporting pupils. As the programme develops, the engagement with parents, carers and other support professionals will benefit from the learning in the application of this element. Parent networks are also invited to join this endeavour.

References

Alkin M (ed.), Encyclopedia of educational research (6th edn). New York: Macmillan.

Catsambis, S. (2001), 'Expanding knowledge of parental involvement in secondary education: Connections with high school seniors' academic success', *Social Psychology of Education*, vol. 5: 149–177.

Department for Education and Skills (2004), *Every Child Matters*, Nottingham: DfES.

De Fraja, G., Oliveira T., et al. (2010), 'Must Try Harder: Evaluating the Role of Effort in Educational Attainment', *The Review of Economics and Statistics* 92(3): 577–597.

Desforges, C. and Abouchaar A. (2003), *The Impact of Parental Involvement, Parental Support and Family Education on Pupil Achievement and Adjustment: A Literature Review*, Department of Education and Skills.

Epstein, J., L. (1992), School and family partnerships. In M. Alkin (ed.), Encyclopedia of educational research (6th edn). New York: Macmillan: 1139–1151.

Epstein, Joyce L. (1995), School/family/community partnerships caring for the children we share. Phi Delta Kappan 76:, 701–712.

Erion, J. (2006), 'Parent Tutoring: A Meta-Analysis', *Education and Treatment of Children* 29(1): 28.

Evangelou, M., Brooks, G. and Smith, S. (2007), 'The Birth to School Study: evidence on the effectiveness of PEEP: an early intervention for children at risk of educational under-achievement', *Oxford Review of Education*, vol. 33, no. 5, pp. 581–609.

Flouri, E. (2006), 'Parental interest in children's education, children's self-esteem and locus of control, and later educational attainment: Twenty-Six Year Follow-Up of the 1970 British Birth Cohort', *British Journal of Educational Psychology*, vol. 76, no. 1, pp. 41–55.

Flouri, E. and Buchanan, A. (2004), 'Early father's and mother's involvement and child's later educational outcomes', *British Journal of Educational Psychology*, vol. 74, no. 2, pp. 141–153.

Goodall, J., Vorhaus, J. et. al (2011), *Review of Best Practice in Parental Engagement*, Nottingham: DfE.

Gorard, S., Huat See, B. and Davies, P. (2012), *The impact of attitudes, aspirations on educational attainment and participation*, York: Joseph Rowntree Foundation.

Hango, D. (2007), 'Parental investment in childhood and educational qualifications: Can greater parental involvement mediate the effects of socioeconomic disadvantage?' *Social Science Research*, 36, 34: 1371–1390.

Harris, A. and Goodall J. (2007, *Engaging Parents in Raising Achievement. Do Parents Know They Matter?* Department for Children, Schools and Families.

Humphrey, N. and Squires, G. (2011), *Achievement for All: National Evaluation Final Report*, Nottingham: DfE.

Kloosterman, R., Notten, N., Tolsma, J., Kraaykamp, G. (2011), 'The effects of parental reading socialisation and early school involvement on children's academic performance: A panel study of primary school pupils in the Netherlands', *European Sociological Review*, vol. 27, issue 3, June: 291–306.

Lamb, B. (2009), *Lamb Inquiry: Special educational needs and parental confidence*, DCSF.

Nutbrown, C., Hannon, P. and Morgan, A. (2005), *Early Literacy Work with Families*, Sage Publications.

Nye, C., Turner, H. et al. (2006), 'Approaches to Parental Involvement for Improving the Academic Performance of Elementary School Children in Grades K-6' *Education Coordinating Group*, The Campbell Collaboration.

O'Brien, M. and Shemilt, I. (2003), *Working fathers: Earning and caring*, Manchester: Equal Opportunities Commission.

OECD (2011), What can parents do to help their children succeed in school? *PISA in Focus 10*.

Peters, M., Seeds, K. et al. (2007), 'Parental Involvement in Children's Education 2007', London: Department for Children, Schools and Families.

Sylva, K., Scott, S. et al. (2008), 'Training Parents to Help Their Children Read: A randomised control trial', *British Journal of Educational Psychology*, vol. 78, no. 3: 435– 455.

Topor, D., Keane, S., Shelton, T. and Calkins, S. (2010), 'Parent involvement and student academic performance: A multiple mediational analysis', *Journal of Prevention & Intervention in the Community*, vol. 38, no. 3, pp. 183–197.

6 Wider outcomes

Introduction – the benefits of wider provision

Research shows that when children engage in wider activities they have higher academic achievement (Catterall, 2012; Metsapelto and Pulkkinen, 2012; Ofsted, 2008) and improved well-being (Ofsted, 2008). Regrettably, for children with SEND, they often do not access the wider provision; this is equally true for other vulnerable groups (LAC and those on FSM). Evidence from the Achievement for All pilot showed that children and young people with SEND were less likely to access extra-curricular opportunities provided by schools than their peers (Humphrey and Squires, 2011). This is also supported by the wider literature; in the USA, Carter et al. (2010) highlight the opportunities missed by high-school students with disabilities (this includes building relationships with peers and developing leadership skills) because they do not access the wider provision.

In many schools in England, wider provision is often seen as an 'add-on' to the main curriculum and can be relatively underdeveloped. This was supported by the Ofsted report *Learning Outside the Classroom* (2008), which highlighted the variability in all aspects of provision. Where provision was 'good', the report provided strong evidence for greater engagement of children in their learning, their higher achievement and better well-being, when they are involved in extra-curricular activities. However, for maximum benefit, the report highlighted the need for activities to be an integral part of the curriculum, planned to support other learning and well evaluated. This also reflects element four of the Achievement for All approach, where schools work with the achievement coach to identify, plan and integrate wider provision for children with SEND, LAC, those receiving FSM and other vulnerable learners. Evidence from both the Achievement for All pilot (Humphrey and Squires, 2011) and the national roll-out of the programme has shown the benefits of wider provision across schools.

Element four of the Achievement for All framework aims to support the participation and enjoyment of pupils in all elements of school life; evaluation of the effectiveness of this element is centred on pupil well-being. Evidence shows that poor pupil well-being is often reflected in their attendance, behaviour and relationships with others at school. The recent Children Society Report (2012) found that children who were repeatedly bullied (that is, more than three times in the last three months) were significantly more likely to experience low well-being (36%) than those that had never been bullied (6%). Sadly, these indicators also have a negative impact on children's engagement with learning, attainment and progress. Founded on an evidence base of what works for children in the area of improving their wider outcomes, Achievement for All developed a framework for schools to effectively implement and develop this element of the programme. It is implemented across the following five key areas:

- Improving attendance.
- Improving behaviour.
- Eliminating bullying.
- Developing positive relationships with others.
- Increasing participation in all aspects of the school and the community including participation in extra-curricular activities.

EVIDENCE FOR WIDER PROVISION

Much of the existing research literature in the field of wider or extra-curricular activities comes from international studies, particularly from the USA and is focused on high-school (secondary level) pupils. Recent studies highlight the positive benefits to children and young people's achievement when they engage in extra-curricular activities. Catterall et al. (2012) explored the benefits for 'at risk' youth of engaging in arts programmes in the USA. Using data from four large national, longitudinal databases, the researchers found that disadvantaged children and young people who engaged both with arts programmes and learning reached levels of academic achievement closer to or greater than the national population studied.

Knifsend and Graham (2012), also in the USA, using a sample of 864 multi-ethnic, high-school pupils (eleventh and twelfth grade) explored the impact of participation in extra-curricular activities on pupil sense of belonging at school and academic engagement and achievement. They also considered the extent (number of activities) and length (time spent) of involvement across four areas: academic/leadership groups, arts activities, other clubs, and sports. Their findings showed that when students were involved in two areas only they had a stronger sense of belonging at school and higher achievement on point scores in eleventh grade and better academic engagement in twelfth grade. Involvement in more than two activities showed a nonlinear relationship, suggesting that involvement in too many extra-curricular activities may have a negative impact on student outcomes.

Findings from research carried out by Fredericks (2012), which also considered the breadth and intensity of extra-curricular activities in which students partici-pated, showed the general falling off in academic achievement when students were involved in more activities. On average, the researcher found that tenth grade students participated in two to three hours of extra-curricular activities for five hours per week. Using data from the Educational Longitudinal Study of American high-school students (sample size: 13,130), Fredericks found that when tenth grade students (15 years old) had moderate engagement with extra-curricular activities, there was a positive association with maths test scores and grades and raised educa-tional expectations at twelfth grade (17 years old). However, her findings showed that when students did more activities for longer periods of time there was a decrease in 'academic adjustment'.

In Finland, a three-year longitudinal study with a relatively moderate sample of 281 children aged nine to ten explored the impact of participation in extra-curricular activities on children's socio-emotional behaviour and academic achievement (Metsapelto and Pulkkinen, 2012). Findings showed that, when children participated in arts, crafts and music activities, they had better attainment in maths, reading and writing. They also had greater concentration, perseverance and took more care over their work (working skills); when children participated in extra-curricular drama they also had better working skills. Findings further showed that when children participated in academic clubs, they were less likely to inter-nalise problems and their academic performance improved. Recent data analysis of student participation in extra-curricular science across OECD (Organisation for Economic Co-operation and Development) countries and economies also highlights better academic performance (OECD, 2012). Findings also showed that in most countries, where students participated in extra-curricular science activities, they had a stronger self-belief in their ability to do science and had greater enjoyment of the subject.

The research cited here provides positive evidence for the engagement of children and young people in wider activities, but may suggest caution in taking part in too many.

WIDER OUTCOMES – CASE STUDIES

Through Achievement for All, participation in school clubs and activities is encouraged as a means of developing self-esteem and the skills needed to work with others. Many Achievement for All schools have considered what is available for all pupils, an outcome has been the creation of a programme of fully inclusive activities. This supports the participation, enjoyment and achievement of pupils in all elements of school life.

What headteachers say

> By supporting the participation, enjoyment and achievement of pupils in all elements of school life, this element of the programme involves key actions to encourage the development of personal skills, characteristics and attributes that will enable pupils to enjoy their childhood and participate fully in the life of their school, their community and wider society. This is achieved through the curriculum and/or through wider involvement in extra-curricular and community activities. (Bexley Academy)

> It's about giving pupils opportunities to shine in other ways and develop their strengths in other things, but also providing activities that will develop confidence – I think that's a big thing. (Achievement for All lead)

The following case studies provide clear and effective examples of how schools have implemented wider outcomes and the impact this has had on target pupils and across the school.

Improving attendance

Case study: Carlton Primary School, Camden

Context
Carlton Primary is an Achievement for All pilot Quality Mark school situated in a challenging inner-city location. Persistent absenteeism was a problem for the school, particularly for children with SEND. There was particular concern with eight hard-to-reach families.

Key challenges
To improve attendance and embed Achievement for All.

Approach
Carlton paid the attendance officer for an extra hour a day to call up any pupils immediately when they were late for school to investigate why and challenge those reasons. The school also started a 'walking bus' for the most persistent late attenders and absentees – a TA was designated to collect these pupils from their homes and take them to a breakfast club which can cater for 40 children. This work was supported with structured conversations, follow-ups with the families and with the family support worker.

Outcomes
One year later persistent absenteeism was brought down to be broadly in line with the national average and fixed-term exclusions had greatly reduced.

Impact
The school also found that this consistent approach allowed them more time to drill down to those few pupils of most concern and look at specific strategies to deal with them.

Case Study: Hampstead School, Camden

Key challenge
To improve attendance.

Approach
A number of students were identified as poor or late attenders and a number also identified as at risk. The school set up an 'early riser club' – a breakfast club – for targeted students. Those on FSM receive this free; for other students there was a cost of 50p for breakfast. The facility is provided in a dedicated room attached to the SEND

curriculum support office and consultation area. The club opens between 7.30–8.30 a.m. and is staffed by a higher level TA together with another member of staff. Around 20–25 students can be accommodated. There is a range of light breakfasts available – cereal, toast, eggs, fruit and drinks. Students help prepare their own breakfast and are responsible for washing up. There are computers and a TV, games such as Connect 4 and card games and plenty of desks and seats.

Students are targeted via a number of routes – those who have poor attendance or are persistently absent. Heads of year also identify students who may be vulnerable for a number of reasons. Older students are encouraged to help younger students and a number of pupils with Down's syndrome are included within the mix.

The school negotiated with the caterers and agreed that the provision would sit separately from their operation and be available for targeted pupils only. A small budget was set aside to buy a lockable food cupboard and cleaning equipment. Two extra hours of TA time per day was assigned to cover staffing.

Outcomes

For many pupils, the club provided a safe haven and helped pupils to be ready for learning. One such person is a Year 7 girl, Pupil D. She took a long public bus journey into school and had to leave home at 7 a.m. Prior to the breakfast club she was not having any breakfast and was left hanging around outside school until opening time. She now attends the 'early riser club' where she meets with friends, has breakfast, and can check her homework.

This is not the only way the club helped to support pupils in their learning. Across pupils who attended, there was a significant improvement in staff/pupil relationships through constant casual 'out of classroom' meetings. For example, Pupil N, a Year 11 boy, caused disruption in class and would ignore the TA assigned to help him. The TA started to help occasionally in the breakfast club and they developed a constructive relationship.

Constructive relationships were also built between pupils. They were more likely to help each other to overcome difficulties and form friendships. For example, Pupil P, a Year 7 boy with poor and often aggressive behaviour, was 'taken on' by Pupil G, a Year 9 boy who was significantly bigger than him. Pupil G had attended the breakfast club for a while and had a calm discussion with Pupil P, questioning him on his behaviour and discussing with him how to deal with difficult or frustrating situations.

Impact

Overall, among the pupils in the 'early risers club', persistent absenteeism fell significantly and staff reported better behaviour and engagement in lessons from targeted pupils.

Improving behaviour

Case study: Carlton Primary School, Camden

Context

Carlton Primary is an Achievement for All pilot Quality Mark school situated in a challenging inner-city location. At Carlton 40% of pupils are identified as SEND and have significant BESD. There are 28 languages spoken in the school. Poor attendance for pupils with SEND has been an issue. The school has its own early years family support worker managing a parenting centre as well as sharing the Family Support Worker (FSW) under the Education Action Zone project.

Approach

Using detailed analysis of data, the school challenged their assumptions about the children within the school, and wanted to understand the link between the lowest attaining children versus those identified with SEND and for each, the impact of language and communication issues together with BESD. The school looked at the relationships between the school and parents, and introduced more constructive conversations with parents, many of whom had poor experiences themselves with schooling. Carlton also looked at the quality of teaching and introduced a Quality First approach with more links between year groups and used peer observation. An example of how the school used this approach follows.

Pupil L, a Year 5 pupil, had difficulty controlling her anger and had other emotional issues. Her behaviour would disrupt classes and she would pick arguments with other pupils when frustrated. This resulted in Pupil L having friendship problems and being isolated from her peer group. At home, this presented as constant poor behaviour in the family and not wishing to go to school; Pupil L was often absent. Through use of structured conversations, Pupil L and her mother started having regular detailed contact with a designated key teacher. This allowed them to understand the full picture around her behaviour and learning and to agree steps to improve this. The school arranged for a child psychotherapist to work with her, her mother and her teacher, to identify particular triggers and agree strategies; for example, Pupil L would 'check in' with the teacher at the beginning of each day and say how she was feeling. When necessary she had the option of a voluntary 15-minute time-out from the classroom to give her quiet and calm. Her family mirrored this approach at home.

Outcomes

Over time Pupil L's confidence grew and her ability to control her emotions and interact with other children improved. Alongside this her progress in literacy and maths improved greatly – she went from one of the lowest attainers in maths to being in the top group. She learned to explain when she felt frustrated and became excited about going to school. Her mother said:

> *My daughter was having a lot of problems with her emotions, particularly controlling her anger. Rather than channelling it in the right way she would lash out and often have a fight or verbal argument. This then affected her schooling; she spent a lot of time out of the classroom and fell behind, which just made her more angry and frustrated in school. Since our involvement with Achievement for All her attitude towards school has completely turned around. Our relationship and communication with the school is brilliant. She comes home buzzing about what she has learned and it's an absolute pleasure to see her engaged again, when before I was so worried.*

Review questions

- Considering the case study, make a list of all the ways the school has approached improving behaviour.
- How would you approach this in your school?
- Consider also how you might approach improving behaviour for learning.

Eliminating bullying

Case study: Hampstead School, Camden

Context
Hampstead School is an eight form entry inner-city secondary school serving an area to the north of the London Borough of Camden. The school had an anti-bullying policy but did not feel that this was fully embraced by the whole school; there was nothing tangible to demonstrate this in action.

Approach
The school decided to consult with pupils, asking for their input on how to reduce bullying. The key ideas from the consultation that were put into action included:

- Peer mentoring.
- A focus on Year 7s and the transition process.
- Assemblies which dealt with bullying and were held with the help of peer mentors and students.
- Training from in-house and outside trainers as appropriate.
- A big focus around bullying in anti-bullying week.
- Ensuring that students reporting concerns to staff were not identified.

Outcomes
To ensure an anti-bullying policy was built throughout the school and maintained a high profile, heads of year were all pastoral leaders, the safer schools officer was a staff governor, and concerns were fed through to the fortnightly multi-agency forum which the school hosted to identify any pupils of concern.

Twilight sessions were used to help boost staff training in their understanding of bullying. Through student involvement the school was kept up to date on newer concerns such as cyber bullying and Facebook.

Communication home to parents was improved to ensure they were aware of issues of bullying and could help both to prevent it and also to raise any concerns they had with the school. Issues around bullying and safety were included in the parent questionnaire.

Bullying issues were introduced through embedded lesson plans in PSHE and assemblies. The following are examples of how this took place in practice.

Curriculum: Holocaust week
During this themed week, pupils were asked to question what created and constituted a safe environment. They were asked to identify what is a 'friend' and to define the parameters of a good and healthy relationship. They also looked at building resilience, considering ways to improve their own confidence and ability to respond to unhealthy relationships.

Culture: Gang culture

As an inner-city school, Hampstead is in an area where there is gang culture and students are at risk. The school operates a zero-tolerance policy and this is made clear to students and parents.

During a termly 'timetable collapse' day the school focused on gang crime bringing in external agencies and speakers (including prisoners and former gang members) to talk with the students about gang crime. The school health team were involved to educate students on the hazards of inappropriate behaviour.

The school also took an individualised approach when necessary. For example, the school became aware via a report from another student that a Year 9 boy was getting involved in a local gang. The parent, pupil and staff team, including a translator, safer schools officer and pastoral leader, were called into a meeting to identify the problem, highlight this to the parent, and put together a plan to help the pupil. The parent commented that he had never seen staff work so hard around the child.

Impact

Parents and teachers report that bullying is reduced, and students feel safer. It has also been noted that a number of feeder primary schools have also adopted similar approaches as a result of the transition projects.

The school believes that as the anti-bullying project started in 2010 (Years 7, 8, 9 and 10) and involved pupils in the development of ideas, pupils, as they progress through the school, will be fully aware of it. The students continue to input new ideas; for example, they decided that peer mentors will have a distinguishing emblem on their school tie to identify them. The school will continue to introduce themes and training to further embed the process, including looking at restorative justice.

Review questions

- Study the above case study. Outline from the outset to the outcomes how the school reduced bullying.
- How would you go about reducing bullying in your school?

Developing positive relationships with others

Case study: Carlton Primary School, Camden

Context

Carlton Primary is an Achievement for All pilot Quality Mark school situated in a challenging inner-city location. The school identified a link between poor peer-group relationships, learning difficulties and learning outcomes.

Approach

The school looked at its after-school club provisions, particularly at which groups of pupils attended which groups. From this, they identified those who didn't attend; pupils identified with SEND featured highly in these figures. Carlton thought about the management and provision of clubs, asked pupils and parents what type of activities they would be interested in and considered how the school could support this.

Outcomes

One child of concern had an interest in drama. The school agreed to part-fund a weekend club out of the area jointly with the parent, with the agreement that the pupil had to attend other learning programmes. When the pupil was allowed to develop among this peer group, he developed friendships in school more easily and made better learning progress.

Impact

The Achievement for All lead/deputy said:

We now drill down to what we can do to make a difference and look at linking strands of the programme – working with parents to understand the whole issue, applying funding in a more strategic way and monitoring the impact on learning. It's not necessarily about spending money – often it's the better quality of the conversations and relationships that helps make the difference.

Review questions

- Would you consider relationships across the school to be poor, good or neither?
- Identify the members of your school community who bring negativity to school relationships? Why?
- List the ways this could be improved.

Increasing participation in all aspects of the school and the community, including extra-curricular activities

Case study: Frederick Bird Primary School, Coventry

Context

Frederick Bird is a mixed-community primary school in the centre of Coventry. It has 673 on roll, where 76.7% of the pupils are EAL, 13.5% have been identified as SEND and 40.3% are claiming FSM. 46 languages are spoken and 15 translators work alongside the pupils. The school wanted to provide some wider outcomes for 15 pupils in Year 5 with School Action Plus status. Many of the children had attendance issues and struggled to show their capabilities on tasks in school. Many of the children had no opportunities to attend after-school clubs or any sporting opportunities in the community. The issues they presented were often complex: speech and language/communication problems, learning difficulties, attachment disorder, mental health difficulties, behaviour challenges, attendance issues and personal hygiene concerns. Pupils were from many of the 'vulnerable' groups in school, Bengali pupils, White British boys and Gypsy Roma families.

Approach

The school planned a year-long project called 'AfA Active'. Six sporting opportunities were provided during the academic year. The project is still continuing. Every half-term a sporting opportunity is provided on a Saturday morning for the Achievement for All cohorts. The school began with cycling. It was able to use the large school site for the first part of the project. During the morning of the activity the school also provided drinks and snacks or a 'second breakfast'. In the first half-term the children achieved their bronze cycling proficiency. Some of the children began the project without being able to ride a bike at all. As an additional unplanned outcome some of the Achievement for All parents had individual adult cycling lessons and learned to ride a bike themselves.

The next opportunity was rambling and orienteering. The school minibus was used to visit sites around Coventry and the West Midlands. Children were taught mapping, rambling and orienteering skills and visited a variety of sites including Oxford Canal and the Burton Dassett Hills. Next was swimming and the children achieved their Level 3 British Swimming Association awards. The children then worked on Basic Life Saving to obtain the 'Rookie Lifeguard' qualification. Other activities include rock climbing, canoeing and sailing.

Outcomes

The school employed specialist teachers for many of the sports and this helped raise the standard of achievement. It introduced independence as a key skill to be practised and taught.

It is considered important to have the same members of school staff to support the project, as families can build relationships with those staff and trust staff. There is obviously the addition of specialist teachers who can be different.

Impact
Overall children's attendance and attitude to learning improved. There was a marked improvement in their attitude to school, and relationships with adults improved. The children worked more readily in teams together and had something important in common. They were more confident to take part in sports in school and are supported by their Achievement for All friends when they do.

Pupils felt confident to suggest to their families that they all take part in a physical activity out of school.

Families developed closer relationships with staff and generally were much more positive about what their children could achieve if given the opportunity.

Case study: Spring Brook Special School, Oldham

Context
Spring Brook is a community primary special school for children (5–11 years) with BESD. Co-located, in a relatively new building, with a mainstream primary school, it also has a duty for outreach into neighbouring schools (for example, it provides places to pupils excluded from other schools and waiting for a place in a mainstream school). Currently with 27 pupils on roll, the majority are boys. The pupils who come to the school are from particularly challenging backgrounds, which includes: coming from one of the two most disadvantaged districts in the borough, having current social services and/or Child and Adolescent Mental Health Services involvement, having varying degrees of care status, coming from homes with no earned income and/or having moderate learning difficulties or social communication difficulties in addition to BESD needs. Through the Achievement for All framework the school particularly wanted to focus on accelerated progress for pupils, BESD, parental engagement and wider outcomes.

Key challenges
The significant challenge to the school was to accelerate the progress of identified pupils. Each of the identified pupils was between one to four years behind age expected levels in each of the three key areas of maths, reading and writing. The school recognised that if pupils were making the expected progress per academic year (two sub levels) then these pupils would still not close the gap and their attainment would remain significantly behind their peers.

The principal aim at the outset of the Achievement for All programme was to enable the identified pupils to make more than two sub levels per academic year and therefore close the gap in attainment with their peers. In addition, the significant BESD needs of the pupils who come to Spring Brook mean that they have often missed huge chunks of learning in their mainstream placement.

Approach

The school staff understood that relationships with the children and families are a key factor in engaging pupils with learning. To build and maintain relationships with previously hard to reach families they established several family/parent activities which continue to be well attended. These include family film night, family club night, parents council, family learning and art afternoons, and parental involvement in lessons.

To further develop the provision for pupils, the school planned memorable experiences into the school curriculum, such as museum visits, living history days, residential holidays and so on. They looked at the extended provision provided by school and ensured that each pupil in school attended an after-school club at least once a week.

They used the SEND communities from which they have often been ostracised. In addition, they worked in collaboration with another school on a Kickstart project. This allowed children and staff to work collaboratively with those from another school in Oldham.

Outcomes

The table below demonstrates the progress made by the four children in the case study over one academic year.

Child/Year group	Reading	Writing	Mathematics
A – Year 6	Working at age appropriate level for a Year 5 pupil (six sub levels progress in one year)	Working at age appropriate level for a Year 4 pupil (two sub levels in one year)	Working at age appropriate level for a Year 6 pupil (four sub levels in one year)
B – Year 6	Working at age appropriate level for a Year 5 pupil (four sub levels in one year)	Working at age appropriate level for a Year 4 pupil (two sub levels in one year)	Working at age appropriate level for a Year 5 pupil (three sub levels in one year)
C – Year 6	Working at age appropriate level for a Year 5 pupil (six sub levels in one year)	Working at age appropriate level for a Year 3 pupil (three sub levels in one year)	Working at age appropriate level for a Year 4 pupil (three sub levels in one year)
D – Year 6	Working at age appropriate level for a Year 5 pupil (three sub levels in one year)	Working at age appropriate level for a Year 5 pupil (three sub levels in one year)	Working at age appropriate level for a Year 6 pupil (four sub levels in one year)

The findings show that after one year each pupil is working at a much more age appropriate level in the three subjects and each pupil made at least two sub levels progress per subject area. Each pupil made three or more sub levels progress in at least one area.

Impact

It is difficult to measure the impact of wider outcomes in isolation from the rest of the work done in school. However, all the activities detailed served to build pupil's self-esteem and confidence and develop relationships as a school community. This in turn impacts on the success felt in the classroom.

Review questions

Consider the two case studies outlined in the context of your school.

- Do you provide extra-curricular activities? List the activities you provide.
- Which pupils attend the activities?
- How could you improve the extra-curricular opportunities you provide for children with SEND, LAC, those in receipt of FSM and other vulnerable learners?

Summary

Through Achievement for All, participation in school clubs and activities is encouraged as a means of developing self-esteem and the skills needed to work with others. Many Achievement for All schools have considered what is available for all pupils, and an outcome has been the creation of a programme of fully inclusive activities. This supports the participation, enjoyment and achievement of pupils in all elements of school life. The programme team are working in partnership with national external organisations to improve and enhance this provision, including Youth Sport Trust, Children's University, the National Orchestra for All and Music First.

References

Carter, E. (2010), 'What are you Doing After School?' Promoting extracurricular involvement for transition-age youth with disabilities, *Intervention in School and Clinic*, vol. 45, no. 5: pp. 275–283.

Catterall, S. with Dumais, S. and Hampton Thompson, G. (2012), '*The Arts and Achievement in at-risk youth: findings from four longitudinal studies*', Washington: National Endowment for the Arts.

Children's Society (2012), *The Good Childhood Report 2012*, The Children's Society.

Fredericks, J. (2012), 'Extra-curricular participation and academic outcomes: Testing the over-scheduling hypothesis', *Journal of Youth and Adolescence*, vol. 41, no. 3: pp. 295–308.

Humphrey, N. and Squires, G. (2011), *Achievement for All: National Evaluation Final Report*, Nottingham: DfE.

Knifsend, C. and Graham, S. (2012), 'Too Much of a Good Thing? How breadth of extra-curricular participation relates to school-related affect and academic outcomes during adolescence', *Journal of Youth and Adolescence*, vol. 41, no. 3: pp. 379–389.

Metsapelto, R. and Pulkkinen, L. (2012), 'Socio-emotional behaviour and school achievement in relation to extra-curricular activity participation in middle childhood', *Scandinavian Journal of Educational Research*, vol. 56, no. 2: 167–182.

OECD (2012),' Are students more engaged when schools offer extracurricular activities?' *PISA IN FOCUS*: OECD.

Ofsted (2008), *Learning Outside the Classroom*, London: Ofsted.

7 Monitoring and evaluation

This chapter is in four sections:

1 Achievement for All and the new Ofsted inspection framework
2 Monitoring
3 Evaluation
4 Achievement for All – how will outcomes for schools be monitored and evaluated?

Introduction – self-evaluation and improvement

Achievement for All is not something that can be made to happen from outside a school or even by the commitment of a few dedicated individuals from the school staff. Achievement for All requires ownership by the headteacher and senior leadership team, governors and all staff (NCSL, 2011). It also requires willingness on the part of schools to analyse their own practice and to identify areas where they could improve.

For the most effective outcomes, Achievement for All will need to be an integral part of whole-school self-evaluation and improvement. In the context of the Ofsted framework, schools will now have self-evaluation frameworks and policies related to SEND, vulnerable and disadvantaged learners.

The following range of tools can be used by schools to assess how well policies are serving different groups of pupils:

- Ofsted's inspection handbook (2012).
- *Evaluating Educational Achievement for All* (Ofsted, 2000).
- *Index for Inclusion* – designed to help schools to assess how inclusive they are and to support their development; it explains the concepts behind

Achievement for All and provides a detailed framework for self-review and materials to support it (Booth and Ainscow, 2004).

- *Quality in Schools* materials (booklet and CD-ROM) – developed by Lloyds TSB and containing tools that a school can use for self-assessment and improvement planning, including self-review in relation to provision for pupils with SEND and Achievement for All.
- Achievement for All needs analysis framework (available on registration).

ACHIEVEMENT FOR ALL AND THE NEW OFSTED INSPECTION FRAMEWORK

September 2012 saw the implementation of the new Ofsted framework making headteachers accountable for accurately identifying and effectively addressing the needs of young learners at risk of under achievement (that is, attainment and progress). When asked by Ofsted inspectors, 'What are you doing to narrow the gap for your pupils with SEND?', headteachers need to provide tangible evidence of their approach and success, including data, analysis, interventions and the views of learners with SEND and their parents.

For Achievement for All schools across England, the changes reflect their practice. These schools have worked in partnership with Achievement for All, rethinking approaches, to improve educational outcomes for vulnerable learners and children with SEND. The success of the impact of the programme on pupil achievement was reaffirmed recently by the 2011 Key Stage 4 results (DfE); in Achievement for All schools, pupils with SEND are progressing faster than the national average for all pupils: three-quarters saw an improvement in Key Stage 4 results compared to two-thirds of schools nationally. In light of the new value added measure, which emphasises rates of progress against pupil intake, the Achievement for All programme is putting many schools ahead in the context of Ofsted.

The impact of Achievement for All on preparing schools for Ofsted has been evidenced by the considerable number and range of improved schools. As the extracts from the new framework on the following pages show, Ofsted emphasise the importance of self review with clear collection and presentation of data, developed teaching and learning, parental engagement and wider outcomes – these are also all central to Achievement for All.

Ofsted inspection (2012)

Changes of emphasis since January 2012

- Effective use of pupil premium funding.
- Sharper focus on children with SEND.
- Sharper focus on literacy (particularly reading).
- Sharper focus on the role of the headteacher and governors particularly in terms of teachers' performance management.

Changes in procedure

The lead inspector will contact the school at 12.00 noon or immediately after on the day before the inspection.

- There are procedures in place for continuing to try to make contact if the school doesn't answer the phone.
- Deferral will be extremely unlikely.
- The inspector should not ask for any information, such as timetables, to be provided in advance, other than a summary of the school's self evaluation, if available.
- There will be no pre-inspection briefing.
- There are no written questionnaires (although the staff questionnaires may be used if the headteacher agrees).
- Parent view will be used (among other sources of evidence) to gauge the view of parents.

Changes in reporting

- The report is short and written in bullet points.
- No letter to pupils.
- If a school requires improvement it will state clearly why it is not good and provide clear ways to help it become good.
- If a school is a good school it will state why it is not yet an outstanding school.

When schools will be inspected

- Outstanding maintained primary and secondary schools will not be routinely inspected unless concerns are identified through risk assessment or otherwise.
- Outstanding schools may still be subject to subject surveys and thematic reviews.
- This includes academy converter schools whose predecessor school was judged outstanding.
- Schools can request an inspection (and pay).
- Residential schools, special schools, PRUs and maintained nursery schools will usually be inspected every three years (unless outstanding at two consecutive inspections).
- A school judged 'good' will usually be inspected within five years.
- A school judged to require improvement will be monitored.
- There will normally be a full inspection within two years.
- If there are three consecutive grade 3 inspections it is 'highly likely' it will be judged inadequate.

How Ofsted will judge schools

Overall effectiveness

- If any one of the four key judgements is inadequate (grade 4), it is likely that overall effectiveness will be inadequate.
- If any one of the four key judgements is 'requires improvement' (grade 3), overall effectiveness will be 'requires improvement'.
- Schools judged 'outstanding' (grade 1) will be expected to have outstanding teaching.
- Achievement is also likely to be outstanding, but exceptionally may be good and rapidly improving.

Four key judgements

These remain the same as in the previous framework:

- achievement
- teaching
- behaviour and safety
- leadership and management.

Overall effectiveness will take into account the four key judgements and how well the school promotes pupils' spiritual, moral, social and cultural development.

The importance of literacy

Overall effectiveness – increased focus on literacy

- Outstanding grade descriptor: there is excellent practice which ensures that all pupils have high levels of literacy appropriate to their age.
- Good grade descriptor: pupils' progress is not held back by an ability to read accurately and fluently. Those pupils who have fallen behind are being helped to make progress in their reading.
- Where pupils' progress in literacy is inadequate, the overall effectiveness is likely to be inadequate.

Achievement – increased focus on literacy

- Outstanding grade descriptor: pupils read widely and often across all subjects.
- Good grade descriptor: pupils read widely and often.

Department for Education definition of progress Key Stage 1–2

Expected progress

- Two levels across four years is equivalent to half a level per year or one and a half sublevels per year (3 APS).

More than expected progress

- At least three levels (or nine sublevels) across four years or three-quarters of a level per year (4.5 APS).

Note

- Pupils who make two sublevels of progress (4 APS) in every year are on track for eight sublevels (almost three whole levels) in four years, so are making at least expected progress and close to making more than expected progress.

- During Key Stage 1, pupils need to make faster progress than during Key Stage 2 to reach the expected level, level 2, by the end of Year 2.

Department for Education definition of progress Key Stage 2–4

Expected progress

- Three levels across five years is equivalent to 1.8 (3.6 APS) or almost two sublevels (4 APS) per year.

More than expected progress

- At least four levels (or 12 sublevels/ 24 APS) across five years (4.8 APS a year).
- Pupils who make two sublevels (4 APS) of progress in every year are on track for ten sublevels (20 APS – just over three levels) of progress in five years, so are making at least expected progress although not quite making more than expected progress.

Closing the gaps

Achievement has an increased focus on closing the gaps in attainment and progress between all pupils nationally and those who:

- are supported through the pupil premium
  - LAC
  - pupils known to be eligible for FSM
  - children of services families
- are disabled
- have SEND.

Achievement

- In evaluating pupils' progress, inspectors should have regard to their starting points in terms of their prior attainment and in relation to their age.
- For those groups of pupils whose cognitive ability is such that their attainment is unlikely ever to rise above 'low', the judgement on achievement should be based on an evaluation of the pupils' learning and progress relative to their starting points at particular ages, and any assessment measures held by the school. Evaluations should not take account of their attainment compared with national benchmarks.

Lower attaining pupils

For pupils attaining below level 1 at the end of Key Stage 1 or 2, inspectors need to use the Progression Materials. The median indentified in 2009 within the Progression Materials is taken as expected progress.

Inspection activities

- Observations of lessons and other learning activities.
- Scrutiny of pupils' work to assess standards, progress and the quality of learning of pupils currently in the school.
- The school's own records of pupils' progress, including the progress of pupils who attend off-site alternative provision for all or part of the week.
- Discussions with pupils about their work.
- The views of parents, pupils and staff.
- Discussions with staff and senior leaders.
- Case studies of individual pupils (local authority and pupil premium).
- Listening to pupils read – particular focus on weaker readers.

Possible questions for the SENCO

- How well are SEND pupils achieving? Has this changed? How do you know?
- How do you check the impact of interventions?
- Do you have a PM objective around this?
- How does the headteacher work out how much progress LAC children should make?
- How do you know the moderation process is robust? Give examples.
- Ofsted says that pupils with SEND should be compared to all pupils nationally. On this measure, how does your data look?
- What is your tracking showing compared with national matrices – expected, more than expected, upper quartile for P level students?

Focus on teaching

- **Good** schools will be expected to have **good** teaching and effective systems for improving it.
- There is no expectation that teachers will teach in a prescribed way.
- The focus is on engagement and progress.

- Observation of lessons will be supplemented by a range of other evidence to evaluate impact of teaching on learning over time.
- Inspectors will consider the extent to which teachers standards are being met.
- Inspectors must evaluate the use that is made of TAs and other adults.

Judging the quality of teaching

Inspectors must consider whether:

- Work is challenging enough for all pupils and meets their individual needs.
- Pupils' responses demonstrate sufficient gains in their knowledge, skills and understanding, including literacy and mathematics.
- Teachers monitor pupils' progress in lessons and use the information well to adapt their teaching.
- Teachers use questioning and discussion to assess the effectiveness of their teaching and promote pupils' learning.
- Pupils understand well how to improve their work.

Focus on performance management

Inspectors will evaluate the extent to which:

- Performance management and other strategies are used to improve teaching.
- Underperformance is tackled.
- Professional development is focused on the identified needs of staff.
- Performance management, appraisal and salary progression are linked.

Increased focus on governance

Ofsted will consider how well governors:

- Hold the headteacher and other senior leaders to account for the achievement, behaviour and safety of all pupils, particularly those who are disadvantaged.
- Use the pupil premium funding and other resources to overcome barriers to learning, including reading, writing and mathematics.
- Use performance management, including of the headteacher, to lever up quality.

Key links with Achievement for All

- Use of the pupil premium and SEND funding.
- Increased focus on the provision and outcomes for pupils with SEND.
- Increased focus on literacy (particularly reading) and mathematics.
- Teachers performance management – pupil progress.

MONITORING

Monitoring is an essential stage in strategic and operational planning, requiring detailed consideration by school, middle and classroom leaders. Having developed and implemented the Achievement for All framework, a critical element of the framework will be the monitoring and evaluating of individual pupil, class and school progress. If plans are not monitored, it is not possible to determine whether the objectives have been achieved. Monitoring will also enable all leaders to obtain the best results from the framework and will also ensure that the Achievement for All framework is set within the school's development/improvement plan. At the heart of the process will be the setting of targets and objectives. Everard et al. (2004, p. 284) underlines the need for 'yardsticks' by which to recognise when the objectives have been achieved and which can be used 'to set a ratchet to prevent backsliding'.

Monitoring is critical to the successful implementation of plans at any level of practice; strategic or operational. Effective monitoring, which also includes 'managing the processes needed to take corrective action in case of a shortfall' (Everard et al., 2004, p. 285), will enable leaders to obtain the best results from the available resources. The process of monitoring will enable leaders and their teams to achieve the agreed Achievement for All objectives. From clear objectives comes a sense of purpose. It may be difficult to obtain co-operation and agreement when working through objectives; however, it is important to reach agreement within a team if the plan is to work effectively. Once objectives have been agreed, pupils, teachers, parents, leaders and wider support agencies can move forward with confidence. It is important to note that monitoring is an ongoing activity and is integral to teaching and learning: it should not be left to the end of the year. At the same time, 'plans cannot be revised too often or they lose their value as a secure basis for planning' (Fidler, 2002, p. 20).

The figure below illustrates the process of monitoring a plan's progress. It is made easier if objectives are clear and practical and agreed by all members of the team (see Chapters 4 and 5).

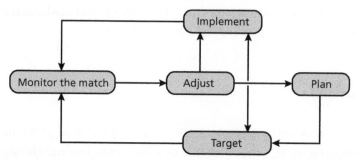

Source: Hargreaves, 1995.

Monitoring Achievement for All will also provide the basis for evaluating practice, enabling pupils, teachers, parents, leaders and wider support agencies to measure and compare performance against shared criteria and to consider the appropriateness of continuing with the plan. Everard et al. (2004, p. 285) advocate setting up, 'as part of the overall plan for change', some means of both 'gathering reliable information and analysing it... in order to measure if the change has been effective and has become truly assimilated'. They highlight the 'future scenario description' as a means of ascertaining the appropriate measures to employ. In addition, they suggest that the following techniques can be used as a means of measuring success, where the emphasis is on the 'actual outcomes of the change':

- a checklist of procedures
- a questionnaire about role responsibilities
- an analysis of exam results or an attitude survey to be completed by those most likely to know if the change has been successful, for example, the pupils.

Most significantly, monitoring will provide a framework in which staff can reflect on their own practice, an outcome of which is enhanced learning.

Leadership and practitioner questions

Consider the following questions in light of the pupil premium:

- Have you clearly identified target pupils?
- Do you have robust assessment systems in place?
- Do you use robust tracking systems for each pupil?
- Do you set clear targets for each pupil?
- Do you monitor progress in English and maths frequently? (E.g. half termly, termly etc.)
- Who is monitoring what, in which ways and with what effectiveness?
- How does monitoring and evaluation relate to the Achievement for All framework?
- Who is responsible for adjusting what, in which ways, when and with what effectiveness?
- Are pupils, teachers, parents, leaders and wider support agencies in agreement? (Is this recorded?)

Planning to monitor Achievement for All

Leaders, teachers and support professionals will need to assess the relationship between individual pupil needs (targets) and school aims (SIP). Resources (people, time, equipment, space) will need to be allocated appropriately and plans monitored according to the most beneficial use of internal and external expertise. Leaders must ask:

- Who will need to be involved?
- How will this impact on current roles?
- Where is the capacity to deliver Achievement for All?

During this process, leaders, teachers and support professionals will also need to look for development opportunities for monitoring and evaluation available from external agencies. These opportunities will need to be analysed with care. Leaders must ask:

- What is the evidence base for such practice?
- Is there a record of impact?
- What is the cost of working with external agencies?
- Is there capacity within the staff?

Monitoring should provide the basis for evaluating teaching practice and learning outcomes on individual pupils. Leaders, teachers and support professionals will be able to measure and compare their performance against agreed criteria. Monitoring will assist leaders in the planning of staff development by providing an insight into the strengths and weaknesses in their departments/teams. This, in turn, should lead to the sharing of good practice. Leaders should consider the following:

- Who monitors the school in action? (Classroom, groups, individuals.)
- How is the monitoring carried out?
- How are the governors and parents informed of the outcomes? (Classroom, groups, individuals.)
- Who prepares the final report?
- How is this disseminated? (Classroom, groups, individuals.)

Practice

In the broadest terms, if policy and practice are not monitored it will not be possible to determine whether objectives have been achieved. Monitoring and evaluation is critical to the successful implementation of a policy for Achievement for All. This will involve senior and leadership teams, teachers, TAs, parents, pupils, governors, academy boards and the local authority (as appropriate).

The process of monitoring will enable members of the school community to move further towards their agreed objectives. Having adopted a collegial approach to policy development, monitoring and evaluation, the school community can move forward with confidence. A shared vision, strong collaboration, shared communication and whole-school commitment are critical to the success of Achievement for All. Monitoring and evaluation processes must be based on practice and outcomes, and related to agreed criteria/set targets. Furthermore, monitoring and evaluation should provide a framework, whereby leaders, teachers and support professionals can reflect on their own practice and professional needs.

EVALUATION

Evaluation is a component of development planning and an essential prerequisite to preparing any subsequent plan. Thirty years ago the DES (1989, p. 17) provided a useful starting point, explaining that the purpose of evaluating plans is to:

- Examine the success of the implementation of the plan.
- Assess the extent to which the school's aims have been furthered.
- Assess the impact of the plan on pupils' learning and achievement.
- Decide on how to discriminate between successful new practices throughout the school.
- Make the process of reporting easier.

It is clear that the process of evaluating the impact of a plan on practice is critical to the successful implementation of the plan. The process of implementing a plan and its impact needs to be evaluated. It is also useful to heed the advice of Everard et al. (2004, p. 285) who suggest that an evaluation will highlight any 'unforeseen consequences of the changes which can subsequently be managed or 'made the subject of further change'.

Evaluating the Achievement for All programme

In contrast to monitoring, evaluation encompasses reviewing the status of a plan's objectives. Through the evaluation process, managers will determine the need to change objectives, priorities and/or practice. As Hall and Oldroyd (1990, p. 34) explained, evaluation is a collaborative exercise involving:

- asking questions
- gathering information
- forming conclusions
- making recommendations.

Hargreaves and Hopkins (1991) stressed the importance of evaluation in enhancing the professional judgement of teachers on the development of teaching and learning. Evaluation can therefore lead to a change in teachers' perception of their practice. Achievement for All has improved pupil learning by changing the behaviours of teachers.

For leaders the evaluation of plans can provide the basis for action in terms of resourcing, curriculum (development and delivery) and engagement with parents, teachers, pupils and wider professionals. Prior to investing in the process leaders will need to review the purpose of the evaluation process.

Review questions

- If plans are not monitored it is not possible to determine whether objectives have been achieved. What techniques would you employ to measure the success of a plan?
- Why is monitoring a plan an essential aspect of leadership in the classroom, department or school?
- How can evaluation enhance teaching and/or learning?
- How can evaluation impact on all pupils?

Once agreed that there is a need to proceed, the following checklist will assist in developing the approach:

Checklist: planning and evaluation

1 Purposes, broad guidelines, aims or objectives for the area under scrutiny which are:
  - clear
  - indicators of desired performance or outcomes.
2 Questions which are:
  - unambiguous
  - penetrating
  - useful.
3 Information which is:
  - accessible
  - related to questions
  - not too voluminous to handle.
4 Conclusions which consider:
  - conditions
  - effects
  - assumptions
  - alternatives.
5 Reports which are:
  - concise
  - focused on readers' need
  - likely to inform decision making.
6 A good evaluation brief:
  - specifying much of the above.

Evaluation reporting and dissemination

The final stage in the Achievement for All evaluation process is to report the outcomes. It will be important to consider the purposes of the report as required, against the original goals, context and rationale. At this point leaders will need to consider and report:

- What was the purpose/ rationale?
- What is the context?
- What is the content?
- What has been the process? Has this met the needs of parents, pupils, leaders, teachers and wider professionals?
- What are the outcomes against the goals?
- Have there been any unintended outcomes? (positive and negative)

Before disseminating the report, a leader will need to reflect on each process and ensure that only necessary and relevant information is presented.

ACHIEVEMENT FOR ALL – HOW WILL OUTCOMES FOR SCHOOLS BE MONITORED AND EVALUATED?

A range of qualitative and quantitative data will be shared with the achievement coach, so that, together, the school champion and achievement coach can make judgements about the impact of the framework on pupil progress and achievement across academic and wider outcomes and also the impact on the engagement of parents and carers. The achievement coach and school champion will together look at termly progress data for reading, writing, maths, behaviour and attendance. This data will be used to evaluate the impact of the framework on academic progress. No information about individual pupils will be removed from the school. Data analysis of groups will identify the impact on progress across wider outcomes and the extent to which the framework has succeeded in its overall aims.

The Achievement for All needs analysis: implementing the programme and the framework

In the first stage of implementing the Achievement for All framework, the school champion (member of the school leadership team), in collaboration with their senior leadership team and the achievement coach, will carry out a needs analysis to determine the school's priorities at the beginning of the school's Achievement for All journey and to plan the route towards achieving the Quality Mark. The needs analysis is based on Achievement for All Quality Standards (details available following registration), which are the processes that schools embed in order to achieve the accelerated progress necessary to meet the Quality Mark criteria. The needs analysis is a self-evaluation by the school against the Quality Standards, designed to be a dynamic document that will be revisited regularly throughout the two years of the Achievement for All programme. The needs analysis is completed during the achievement coach's second visit and schools are asked to give consideration to their judgements in preparation for this meeting. The needs analysis will support:

- Overall planning and implementation of the framework; specifically the activities that the achievement coach will lead over the following sequence of visits.
- Identification of areas of focus for element four (wider outcomes).
- Identification of any staff professional development needs.
- Monitoring of the impact of the framework by establishing a baseline position.

How does the Achievement for All programme monitor the effectiveness of the framework?

The Achievement for All regional leads and achievement leads carry out joint visits to schools with achievement coaches to monitor the progress of Achievement for All and to gather feedback on the framework as a whole. Achievement for All 3As also sends out a twice-yearly school champion survey to gain feedback on how schools feel about the impact of the programme and how the framework can be improved.

Case study: North Chadderton, Oldham

Context

North Chadderton, a large foundation school with a sixth form, has Quality Mark Achievement for All status. It is a Business and Enterprise College and has a Healthy Schools Award. In 2011 11.6% of pupils were claiming FSM and 5% of pupils had been identified as SEND; both below the national average. The proportion of students gaining 5+ A*–C grades including English and maths increased from 51% to 67% between 2009 and 2011. The proportion of students making expected progress in English and maths in 2011 was above the national average of 58.2%.

The senior leadership team believed that expectations for SEND pupils across the school were low. Developing meaningful targets for these pupils was difficult as data analysis lacked the necessary detail. The senior leadership team believed Achievement for All would provide the framework needed to raise expectations and attainment across the school. In addition, they wanted to bring greater focus across the four elements of leadership, teaching and learning, parental engagement and wider outcomes (particularly regarding exclusions).

Approach

The school appointed an operational lead to embed Achievement for All processes and practices within their systems. To achieve this, the operational lead worked closely with the SENCO and other senior members of the staff team, including year heads and departmental heads. The team focused on how best to support vulnerable pupils – developing structured conversations, providing small-group classes and supporting pupils in more focused groups to embed learning. The school also worked on raising expectations in all lessons with more focus on interventions and a greater concentration on use of data, setting aspirational targets and greater accountability in the classroom.

The following provides an outline of how the school evaluated the Achievement for All programme once implemented and the lessons learned as a result:

Evaluating the impact of different provisions on pupil progress: method
- Identified key questions.
- Set up the following focus groups: pupils, identified because they needed additional support/were not on track/were LAC/FSM/on the SEN register; parents; TAs following responses to a questionnaire completed by all TAs and a range of 'inclusion' staff – pastoral leaders, school counsellor, manager of the internal isolation unit, and attendance officer.
- Conducted a thorough analysis of data for all pupils on the Additional Needs Register to check progress towards targets.
  - Scrutinised a sample of books for the pupils in the focus group.
  - Conducted mini lesson observations (around 20 minutes each) to observe pupils in the focus group and each TA at least once.

Evaluating the impact of different provisions on pupil progress: outcomes
- There was not enough differentiation in lessons.
- The TAs had a big impact on pupils' social and emotional needs, but not on pupils' attainment.
- Pupils were very positive in their view of how the TAs helped them in lessons and very positive relationships were noted.
- Interventions were not being analysed to assess whether they had impact and some interventions were not being sufficiently exploited.
- Pupils did not have a clear enough picture of what their targets were and more specifically how they could reach them. TAs had only limited knowledge of what was specifically needed to help pupils make progress.
- A re-assessment of how the TAs are deployed was necessary to facilitate working more closely with teaching staff and being involved in lesson planning/adaptations to schemes of work, progress interviews, and so on.
- CPD needed to be more personalised to meet individual needs.

Lessons learned – there needs to be:
- Rigorous tracking of pupil progress with provision in place to tackle under-achievement at an early stage.
- The effective deployment of the school workforce to ensure support staff are used in the most effective way to support teaching and learning; all staff should feel accountable for the progress of each child.
- Personalised CPD to meet needs of individual staff/departments, with a focus on high-quality whole-class teaching.
- Effective multi-agency working to enhance the provision.

Summary

Monitoring and evaluation are critical to the successful implementation of Achievement for All. Having implemented the Achievement for All framework, school champions and achievement coaches will need to monitor its progress in collaboration with leaders, teachers, parents, pupils and wider professionals. Monitoring will also enable leaders and teachers to obtain the best results from the available resources. Most significantly, monitoring will enable staff to reflect on their own practice, an outcome of which is enhanced job satisfaction (Humphrey and Squires, 2011).

References

Blandford, S. (2006), (2nd Ed.) *Middle Leadership in Schools: Harmonising Leadership and Learning*, Harlow: Pearson.

Booth, A. and Ainscow, M. (2002), *Index for Inclusion*, Bristol: CSIE.

Department of Education and Science (1989), *Planning for School Development: Advice for Governors, Head teachers and Teachers*, London: HMSO.

Everard, K. B., Morris, G. and Wilson, I. (2004), *Effective School Management*, 4th Ed., London: Paul Chapman Publishing.

Fidler, B. (2002), *Strategic Management for School Development*, London: Paul Chapman Publishing.

Hall, V. and Oldroyd, D. (1990), *Management Self-development for Staff in Secondary Schools, Unit 4: Implementing and evaluating*, Bristol: NDCEMP.

Hargreaves, D. H. (1995), 'Self-managing schools and development planning – chaos or control?' School Organisation, 15(3), pp. 215–17.

Hargreaves, D. H. and Hopkins, D. (1991), *School effectiveness, school improvement and development planning* in Preedy, M. *Managing the effective school*, London: Paul Chapman Publishing.

Humphrey, N. and Squires, G. (2011), *Achievement for All: National Evaluation Final Report*, Nottingham: DfE.

Lloyds TSB (2012), *Quality in Schools Material* (booklet and CD-ROM).

NCSL (2011), *Achievement for All: Leadership Matters*, Nottingham: NCSL.

Ofsted (2012), *Inspection Handbook*, London: Ofsted.

Ofsted (2012), *Framework for Inspection*, London: Ofsted.

Ofsted (2000), *Evaluating Educational Inclusion: Guidance for inspectors and schools*, London: Ofsted.

Ofsted (2013) *School Inspection Handbook: Handbook for inspecting schools in England under Section 5 of the Education Act 2005 (as amended) from September 2012*, London: Ofsted.

8 Looking to the future: sustaining Achievement for All

Introduction

The aspirations and achievements of all of our young people, both in school and in the wider society, are important to us all; whether we are parents, leaders, teachers, policy makers or employers.

As you have read, Achievement for All is a national programme that focuses on improving the aspirations, access and achievement of pupils with SEND, LAC, those receiving FSM and other vulnerable and disadvantaged pupils. This represents around 20% of the pupils in England. However, the programme has been independently shown to make the most of the ability and potential of *all* young people. This chapter outlines the history of Achievement for All 3As, the charity and the programme, and looking to the future considers how Achievement for All is at the centre of educational reform.

ACHIEVEMENT FOR ALL 3AS: THE CHARITY STORY

Our story began in 2008 when Brian Lamb OBE was commissioned by the then Secretary of State for Children, Schools and Families to make recommendations on how to increase the attainment and achievement of young people with SEND.

The recommendations published in the *Lamb Inquiry into Parental Confidence in Special Education Needs* (2009) stated that changes should be made to how SEND is identified in young people, that schools should be more accountable for the progress of low-achieving learners, and that schools should be supported in setting high aspirations for all, focusing on attainment, engaging parents and developing wider outcomes.

These recommendations became the foundations of the Achievement for All charity and programme. In essence, the programme is a framework for whole-school improvement. It is implemented through four key elements: school leadership; teaching and learning (assessment and data tracking); parental engagement; and wider outcomes (such as young people exploring their talents by being involved in extra-curricular activities, for example involvement in music or art).

As explained in Chapter 1, the Achievement for All programme was piloted from 2009 to 2011 in 454 English schools by a group of expert educational professionals, including internationally recognised practitioners, researchers, and academics, led by Professor Sonia Blandford. The pilot programme was evaluated in 2011 by the University of Manchester. This evaluation found that the programme had a significant impact on the progress of young people with SEND in English and maths; a number of the young people with SEND who took part in the programme made better progress in these subjects than the national average of pupils without SEND (37% in English, 42% in maths).

Crucially, the evaluation also found that, while the programme focuses on children with SEND, the positive impact of the programme is felt across the whole school, for the benefit of all young people. The profound outcomes of the pilot provided the motivation for the creation of Achievement for All 3As.

Achievement for All pilot (2009–2011)

Introduced in September 2009, Achievement for All was delivered in 454 primary, secondary and special schools and PRUs across ten local authorities in England. The Achievement for All pilot aimed to increase the attainment and progress, in reading, writing and mathematics of pupils identified with SEND; improve the engagement of their parents with the school and improve wider outcomes for this group of children, including behaviour, attendance and engagement in school activities. The Achievement for All pilot, with a focus on pupil outcomes, embedded a whole-school approach to school improvement. Implemented collaboratively with schools through the key elements of school leadership, teaching and learning, parental engagement and wider outcomes, the initiative, was delivered in partnership by the Department for Education (DfE), National Strategies and the National College (NCSL). Manchester University carried out a full evaluation.

Overview of the evaluation

- 28,000 pupils were involved.
- Quantitative information was studied, including pupil attainment and progress in English and maths, absenteeism data and behaviour reports.
- Qualitative information was drawn from extensive interviews with school leaders, teachers, parents and students.

In evaluating the Achievement for All pilot the University of Manchester had completed one of the largest studies of a programme for children identified with SEND in Europe. To assist with the next stage of the development and roll out of the programme they recommend:

- A strong focus on school-led improvement to transform the outcomes for children with SEND. The most successful schools in the pilot had strong leadership from the headteacher or senior leadership team – rather than relying purely on the SENCO.
- Teachers should carry out regular target reviews with parents to monitor progress of children and assess where extra help may be required.
- Regular, scheduled conversations on educational outcomes between parents and teachers should take place, with teachers given extra training in managing these relationships.
- Achievement for All is most successful when schools build on existing good practice and share ideas between schools.

Policy that transcends changes in Government– Green Paper (SEND)

The aims and objectives of the Achievement for All pilot have remained central to government policy; on 9 March 2011, the SEND Green Paper (DfE, 2011) was published, recommending the Achievement for All programme for schools in England. The Achievement for All programme is seen as the foremost means of delivering school improvement and enhancing educational outcomes for pupils identified as SEND. This was affirmed by supporting documentation of the Children and Families Bill:

> *...we are enabling all schools to benefit from the highly successful Achievement for All approach through our support of the Achievement for All 3 As charity and will reflect the key features of that approach in the Code of Practice.* (TSO, 2013)

Creating the Achievement for All 3As charity – stage 1

By November 2010, Achievement for All 3As was registered as a limited company. Soon after, Sonia Blandford, CEO of Achievement for All 3As approached PriceWaterhouseCoopers (PwC) with a view to developing a partnership to bid for the yet to be agreed national roll-out of Achievement for All. Further discussions ensued and in January 2011, a preliminary agreement was made to develop a partnership. Charity trustees were approached in January 2011 and committed their support for the development of the charity. Teach First supported facility management and health and safety. During this time, Sonia Blandford submitted a bid to J.P. Morgan, securing further core funding (from September 2011).

Achievement for All 3As charity board

In November 2010, Professor Sonia Blandford began discussions with those who would become the founding charity trustees, including Brian Lamb as Chair (Lamb Inquiry, 2009), Dr David Cole (UK Sport), Michael Clark (McKinsey, now ARK), Melanie Warnes (headteacher, The Castle School, PwC headteacher programme), Jo Owen (author and social entrepreneur), and Amanda Timberg (Teach First). Freshfields LLB and J.P. Morgan were also approached as founding sponsors. Bates, Wells and Braithwaite guided staff through the initial legal processes. Achievement for All 3As was registered as a company limited by guarantee, and on 27 May 2011, Achievement for All 3As charitable status was issued.

The objectives of the charity remain central to all activities in schools and the wider community:

1 The advancement of education for the public benefit in particular (but without limitation) for *learners with special education needs and/or disabilities*

and/or from *disadvantaged backgrounds* and providing advice, information and support to their parents or carers.

2 To help young people including by providing support and activities which develop their *skills, capacities and capabilities* to enable them to participate in society as mature and responsible individuals.

Creating the Achievement for All 3As charity – stage 2

On 23 May 2011, Achievement for All 3As charitable status was confirmed. For the first three months charity staff continued to work pro bono (as did Trustees). The core team set up the various aspects of the charity – human resources processes, the finalisation of charity status and governance matters (logo, website and insurance), programme and organisational development (programme, finance and legal), programme development, creation of the website for the charity and setting up the process for registering schools. In June 2011, having completed the bidding process, with funding in place, a bank account was opened.

Recruitment of achievement (national) and regional leads began immediately; interviews were held in May and June.

Developing the Achievement for All programme

At the tender stage and for the first two terms of the programme the charity worked in partnership with PwC who advised on programme management. The various areas of work were split into five key work packages, which continue to provide the framework for risk management and delivery, outlined below:

- Work package 1 – main programme
- Work package 2 – operations and programme management
- Work package 3 – monitoring and evaluation
- Work package 4 – school registration and payments
- Work package 5 – web and community.

Creating the Achievement for All 3As charity – stage 3

By June 2011, the charity had become a going concern and various staff appointments were made, including a finance director, office manager, stakeholder manager, director of IT, materials director, chief operating officer, achievement leads for the south and north, director of business development, support coordinator for the regional leads and research and data manager. Eight regional leads who had led the pilot in their LAs were appointed to the charity administrator schools south in December. As recruitment of schools to the programme expanded, new regional leads were appointed, from senior positions in local authorities and in schools.

From January to September 2011, charity staff and trustees worked pro bono to secure the funding to deliver the national roll-out of the programme and to develop the organisation. This work included:

- Sonia Blandford leading the charity, programme and organisational infra-structure and development.
- Cherry White leading on charity status and governance matters, including in-depth work on developing and agreeing the articles of association and governance structures, as well as the development and submission of the charity application to the charity commission.
- Sue Briggs and Jackie Holderness leading on programme and materials development.
- Nicola Laverton leading on human resources to ensure successful recruitment of a programme team with the educational expertise and geographical spread to deliver a national programme.
- The board members continuing to provide additional support and expertise.

Logistically, the charity required accommodation, a bank account, insurance, office furniture, printing facilities and catering – the following organisations assisted, providing pro bono support, services and equipment: Vodafone, Barclays Ltd, PwC, Warrens Office, Donnington Hotel and Spa, Newbury College, Credit Suisse, Teach First, Hilton Hotels and Freshfields LLB.

The charity became a going concern in June 2011. On 14 June 2011, McKinsey hosted a full day development meeting designed to translate the learning from the pilot to the national programme. At the same time, the recruitment of new schools began.

The 17 July 2011 was a key date in the development of Achievement for All. On that day, Professor Sonia Blandford and Sue Briggs ran the first training session for the achievement coaches that would support the programme. The national roll-out of the Achievement for All programme had begun. At the time of publication it is anticipated that the Achievement for All programme will be delivered in over 2,000 schools supported by 500 headteachers and senior professionals, led by a core team of 50 operational and leadership staff.

THE ACHIEVEMENT FOR ALL PROGRAMME (2011 ONWARDS)

The current national Achievement for All programme (2013) is based on in-depth interaction, dialogue, and co-construction between the staff and leadership of the participant school (including a named school champion drawn from the senior leadership team of the school), and an expert network of Achievement for All coaches.

Our 200 Achievement for All coaches are all highly experienced, outstanding, and in many cases nationally recognised, school leaders and practitioners, including a number of Local Leaders of Educations (LLE) and National Leaders of Education (NLEs). The Achievement for All coaches are supported by 15 regional leads (all of whom are highly innovative and effective teachers, leaders, and practitioners), many of whom had led the pilot in their local authorities.

The partnership between schools, the school champion, and the Achievement for All coaches is designed to:

1 Establish an initial needs analysis and identification of the pupil target group in the school.
2 Support the school in creating and implementing a programme plan, bolstered and informed by a set of bi-weekly half-day visits over two years.
3 Facilitate three whole-school INSET days over two years.
4 Integrate the school into an overlapping set of communities of practice with thousands of other schools.

This partnership working is underpinned by a simple 'virtuous circle' of activity in schools:

- Achievement for All coaches contribute to developing the skills of school staff.
- Achievement for All coaches help school staff to hold effective structured conversations with parents and carers.
- School staff develop their teaching and learning strategies, informed by Achievement for All coaches, which are designed to increase opportunities for the target young people.
- School colleagues evaluate outcomes.
- Outcomes are expanded to all pupils.
- Outcomes are fed into the development of school staff.

Successes reported by the PwC Achievement for All monitoring and evaluation team between September 2011 and December 2012, include the following:

Quantitative

- A closing of the achievement gap – indicated by the range of APS change between the bottom and top performing schools:
  - pupils in the majority of primary schools making better progress than national expectations for *all* pupils
  - an average increase in APS for targeted children (SEND) of over 4.4 for reading, 4.4 for writing and 4.3 in maths, which is above that required by Ofsted for all pupils
  - score changes of 6.7 (reading), 7.4 (writing) and 7.4 (maths) in the top performing school
  - accelerated progress across reading, writing and maths for target pupils in a further 339 schools which had completed their first term of working with Achievement for All.

Qualitative

- Schools operating in a range of contexts, and at different stages of implementation have been enabled to address the specific needs of staff, parents and pupils in their school – the bespoke nature of the programme is perhaps its most unique feature.
- Achievement for All has provided additional impetus for school leaders and teaching staff to focus on low attaining pupils. The programme is being effectively embedded across schools, despite leadership challenges in some schools.
- There is a strong commitment by school leaders to maximise the potential of the programme in terms of its capacity to impact at an individual level, a whole-school level and at a partnership level with other schools.
- Structured conversations continue to be the outstanding success of the programme to date. The conversations are feeding into more effective planning, which is enabling schools to deliver more personalised teaching and learning. In addition, parents and staff are working more effectively together to address the individual needs of each child.
- Schools are beginning to devise bespoke methods of recording and reviewing structured conversations. As schools progress through the programme they

are beginning to explore how the structured conversation tool might be improved and/or applied to other contexts.

- Schools are reporting that as a result of the programme, they are more strategically focused on ensuring high quality teaching and learning. New initiatives are being introduced and schools are working to ensure that staff have the necessary skills, and that good practice is being disseminated.
- The programme is encouraging schools to reap the positive benefits that derive from more effective monitoring and tracking of vulnerable pupils. Schools are investing in new systems and approaches which are enabling them to monitor interventions as well as tracking, analysing and comparing individual pupil and group progress.
- Schools are committed to achieving wider outcomes for pupils and schools consistently express their desire to work towards addressing the needs of the whole child. Wider outcomes to be considered from the start with all elements in parallel to ensure wider outcomes are addressed most effectively.
- Schools are reporting that the programme has encouraged them to focus strategically on planning and implementing additional activities for vulnerable pupils and to identifying gaps in provision.
- As schools progress through the programme, they are beginning to report on the positive benefits for pupils as a result of focussing on wider outcomes in terms of improved attendance, behaviour and particularly self-esteem.

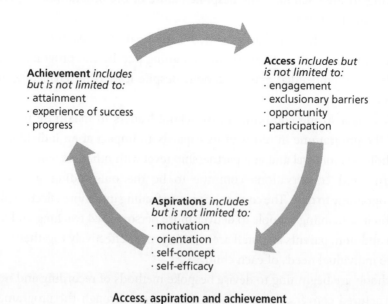

Achievement *includes but is not limited to:*
· attainment
· experience of success
· progress

Access *includes but is not limited to:*
· engagement
· exclusionary barriers
· opportunity
· participation

Aspirations *includes but is not limited to:*
· motivation
· orientation
· self-concept
· self-efficacy

Access, aspiration and achievement

The figure above shows how the particular focus of the Achievement for All programme on aspiration, access and achievement and the interconnection between the three areas.

THE FUTURE

To date, Achievement All has featured in seven government publications:

- 2009 Lamb Inquiry recommending the Achievement for All pilot
- 2010 University of Manchester Interim Report (pilot)
- 2011 University of Manchester findings (pilot)
- 2011 Green Paper – *Support and aspiration: A new approach to special educational needs and disability*
- 2012 Green Paper response – *Support and aspiration: A new approach to special educational needs and disability – Progress and next steps*
- 2013 Children and Families Bill
- 2013 Indicative Code of Practice (DfE).

In addition, the aims, practices, and successes for Achievement for All are allied to many current policy initiatives. For example, on 18 April 2012, the then Children's Minister Sarah Teather announced a £500,000 programme designed to help school support staff to get degree-level and specialist training in helping children with SEND; this being wholly in-tune with the objectives of Achievement for All. On 16 April 2012, the Government's Expert Adviser on Behaviour announced a new initiative on school absence. The evaluation of the Achievement for All pilot concluded that the programme impacted positively on behaviour – including reducing persistent non-attendance by 20%.

In May 2012, the SEND Green Paper progress and response document was published (DfE, 2012), and the success of both the partnership and programme featured as an exemplar of future practice. The programme is also closely aligned with Ofsted, Teaching Schools, New Schools and the expansion of academies.

In November 2012, Edward Timpson, the then Minister for Children and Families announced the extension of funding to Achievement for All 3As, expanding the work of the charity to include LAC and those receiving FSM. In his letter he stated:

> *I have decided to extend funding for the Achievement for All programme, which has led to significant improvements in academic and wider outcomes for pupils with SEN.*

In terms of the future possible impacts of Achievement for All 3As (the charity), the experience and expertise of the charity suggest that the following may be options to contribute to the aspirations, access and achievement of all young people and learners:

- The establishment of a 'resource of first recourse' for teacher professional development related to pupil achievement and SEND (which could potentially contribute to the school support staff scholarship programme).
- International comparisons and the development of country-specific professional development for school leaders and teachers of pupils with SEND and other disadvantaged learners.
- Knowledge-sharing and debate between different national approaches to provision for all students (including those with SEND).
- The embedding of the principles of Achievement for All into 'mainstream' UK provision for all children, young people and learners, including early years settings, all schools and further education in England, Scotland, Northern Ireland and Wales.

Extending our reach – working in partnership

Central to the mission of Achievement for All 3As is to work with and support partner organisations that have a similar mission to ours to improve opportunities and support for schools, pupils and parents in increasing their aspirations, access and achievement. Achievement for All 3As currently works with the following partners:

- Anti-Bullying Alliance
- Autism Education Trust
- Council for Disabled Children
- Communication Trust
- Contact a Family
- CUREE
- Dyslexia SpLD Trust
- Department for Education

- Early Intervention Foundation
- Early Support
- Education Endowment Foundation
- Esmee Fairbairn Foundation
- First News
- Future Leaders
- Greenhouse
- ICAN
- Jamie's Farm
- National Literacy Trust
- Music First
- My Way Campaign (Henry Winkler)
- Place 2 Be
- National Children's Bureau
- National College
- National Association of Special Educational Needs
- National Orchestra for All
- Teach First
- Teaching Leaders
- Youth Sport Trust
- 157 Group

Question: Do you believe in Achievement for All?

For every school, Academy Group or Local Authority, there are at least ten good reasons to join Achievement for All:

1 Closing the achievement gap for pupils with SEND
2 Improving behaviour and attendance
3 Supporting schools in their Ofsted assessments
4 Helping schools meet their increased accountability for the most vulnerable 20%
5 Creating leading schools
6 Improving relationships with parents
7 Delivered by school leaders for school leaders
8 Improving awareness and focus on SEND
9 A programme that meets each school's individual needs
10 Saving money for schools.

Inspired?

If you have been inspired by this book go to www.afa3as.org.uk for more information on how you as a leader, teacher, parent, pupil or wider professional can engage in partnership with Achievement for All 3As.

To Register

Schools can join Achievement for All at key points throughout the year, with a rolling registration ensuring schools can sign up at a time in the school year that best suits them. Schools can register individually or as a consortium. Details are found on the website: http://www.afa3as.org.uk/programme/registration

References

Department for Education (2011), *Support and Aspiration: A new approach to special educational needs and disability*, Nottingham: DfE.

Department for Education (2012), *Support and Aspiration: A new approach to special educational needs and disability – Progress and next steps*, Nottingham: DfE.

Lamb, B. (2009), *Lamb Inquiry into Parental Confidence in Special Education Needs*, Nottingham: DCSF.

Humphrey, N. and Squires G. (2011), *Achievement for All, National Evaluation: Final Report*, Nottingham: DfE.

Humphrey, N. and Squires G. (2011), *Achievement for All, National Evaluation: Interim Report*, Nottingham: DfE.

The Stationary Office (TSO) (2013), Children and Families Bill 2013: Contextual Information and Responses to Pre-Legislative Scrutiny Presented to Parliament by the Secretary of State for Education by Command of Her Majesty: TSO.

Glossary

Access This has a two-fold meaning. The first is the removal of barriers preventing access to learning; these can be broad or specific, e.g. low expectations, physiological, social, environmental, educational and more. The second is the provision of education.

Aspiration This encompasses the expectations, beliefs, understanding and capacity of learners to engage fully and positively in the learning process.

Assessment for Learning Teachers use the information from classroom observation, to involve the children in deciding their learning objectives and how best they can meet them. (First given prominence as a valuable means of raising achievement through the work of Black and Wiliam, 1998).

Collegial approach People working together as a team, sharing ideas, making decisions and deciding together how to implement the decisions made.

Creativity Teaching, which focuses on outcomes, to enable children to think and/or act imaginatively, to generate a new idea. (In education, the most widely accepted definition is that provided by the National Advisory Committee for Cultural and Creative Education (NACCCE 1999). They define it as '*Imaginative activity fashioned so as to produce outcomes that are both original and of value.*' In this context, the process has four dimensions: 'thinking or behaving *imaginatively*; imaginative activity which is *purposeful*: that is, it is directed to achieving an objective; it must generate something *original,* and finally the outcome must be of *value* in relation to the objective'.

Culture This might be defined in terms of the values and beliefs held by individuals, which distinguish them from another group of individuals. Culture is made known through practices (words, greetings, dress, food, religious ceremonies and so on).

Differentiation This relates to the adaptation of the curriculum to meet the learning needs of each child. Differentiation can be by input – where different tasks, determined by a child's ability, are selected by the practitioner prior to the activity – or by output – where all children do the same activity and the differences in the way children carry out and/or complete the activity are considered. (Dr Carol Tomlinson brought the concept to prominence, crystallising her research and thoughts in various articles in the late 1990s.)

Distributed leadership Leaders delegate tasks and responsibility to team members, giving them the authority to make and act on a decision. (Early references to distributed leadership in schools are found in the work of Professor Peter Gronn – late 1990s.)

Early support to improve the delivery of services for disabled children, young people and their families through key working around the child and their families.

Evaluation This encompasses reviewing the status of a plan's objectives. Through the evaluation process, teachers/school leaders will determine the need to change objectives, priorities and/or practice.

Extended schools A school providing services (activities and further educational or health programmes for children, parents, families and the wider community) beyond the school day. In January 2002, the Department for Education and Skills (DfES) and National Union of Teachers (NUT) commissioned NFER to carry out research exploring the 'extended school' model in England (often called community colleges and full service schools). In 2002 the DfES sponsored 25 local authorities to develop extended schools pathfinders. In 2004 the DfES in its document *Strategy for Education* proposed that primary and secondary schools in England become extended schools. The 'prospectus': *Extended schooling: Access to opportunities and services to all* followed in 2005 setting out the vision for extended schools.

Formative assessment Through observation and other means, teachers find evidence for and evaluate pupils learning; using this information and working with the pupils they decide on learning objectives and how best the pupils can meet them. It aims to inform practice.

Free School Meals (FSM) Pupils are eligible for a free meal at school if their parents/carers are in receipt of state support (e.g. income support, job seekers allowance etc.).

Green Paper In England, a green paper is the government's proposal of an action or plan of action. It provides the opportunity for discussion and response.

Helpless-orientation Children who lose focus and concentration, adopting an attitude of failure, when faced by a difficult task.

Improvement Plan (IP) Provides a framework for strategic planning in which staff can identify long- and short-term objectives to manage themselves effectively. An IP should relate to the school's vision or mission, its achievements, government policy and local authority policies and initiatives.

Independent learner A learner who has the belief in him/herself to think through learning activities, problems or challenges, make decisions about his/her learning and act upon those decisions. (The term has different meanings in different contexts including educational phase and culture. It is more frequently associated with students in further/higher education.)

Individual Education Plan (IEP) A teaching and learning plan for pupils with SEN, setting out targets and developed by teachers in partnership with parents to help pupils advance in their learning; actions are additional to what is in place for the class.

Learning dispositions As an inner attitude, this can be developed in a school and predisposes a child to want to and to be able to advance in learning.

Local Leader of Education Headteachers who work in partnership with other headteachers to guide improvement and build capacity for sustained change; they are successful and have a record of supporting other schools.

Long-term plan An overview of the children's learning, covering all areas of the curriculum and detailing when learning areas will be revisited.

Looked After Children (LAC) A legal term, defined by the Children Act (1989) as a child *'looked after by a local authority if he/she is in their care or is provided with accommodation for more than twenty-four hours by the authority'* (DfES, 2006: 3).

Management Sustaining an existing code of practice, with limited authority to change the 'direction' of an organisation.

Mastery-oriented Children who remain confident in attitude and approach towards a difficult task. They believe in their own ability as learners and want to succeed. (The idea of goal-oriented students was first proposed by Eison (1979), the American educational psychologist. This work was followed by Dweck.)

Medium-term plan This is concerned with the curriculum. In essence, it covers a specific area/theme of learning.

Mission statements These set out what a setting's intended outcomes are for its children, their development and overall attainments – academic, social and personal.

Monitoring The means chosen to measure and compare the effect of a particular change against agreed objectives and outcomes.

Motivation Inspiring others to do/carry out and to want to do/carry out what is required or needed.

National Leader of Education An excellent headteacher, who works with key staff in his/her school to share expertise with schools in demanding circumstances; a National Leader of Education will also support other schools in building leadership capacity.

Observational assessment Teachers observing and evaluating children's learning, either as a planned observation or as an incidental observation.

Operational plan This is about tasks underpinned by policies and targets and relates directly to the role of all staff in the setting: who does what, when and how.

Organisational improvement plan A plan aimed at improving the quality of teaching and learning, which focuses on all areas within the setting where improvement is needed. It considers the vision/mission, the values, past achievements and government policy.

Pathfinder An organisation (government/not) or person which/who finds the best or an appropriate approach to a new initiative or way of working. In September 2011, the government announced 20 pathfinders across 31 local authorities to test out the key proposals in the SEN and disabilities Green Paper.

Achievement for All 3As is a Pathfinder Delivery Partner working closely with the organisations.

Performance review Whereby one professional holds him/herself accountable to him/herself in the presence of another professional.

Personalised learning The adaptation of teaching and curriculum to meet the learning needs of the individual child. It is based on the collaborative approach of the teacher, child and his/her parents/carers, where teachers are continuously collecting and evaluating evidence of learning, with a view, through discussion with the child, of engaging him/her in his/her learning to achieve the best possible outcomes for the child both emotionally and academically. (The term was popularised in education by David Hargreaves (2004) in *Personalising Learning: Next Steps in Working Laterally.* London: Specialist Schools and Academics Trust and brought to the forefront by Tony Blair's government. Research has been carried out by the DfES Innovation Unit and National College of School Leadership (2004) and international research published by OECD.)

Pupil premium Additional funding given to schools to increase the achievement (progress and attainment) of disadvantaged pupils. This includes those claiming FSM (including pupils registered at any time in the previous six years) and LAC.

Pupil Referral Unit (PRU) An organisation, supported by the local authority to provide education for pupils excluded from or unable to attend any mainstream school; education is overseen by a teacher in charge (similar to a headteacher), while governance is the responsibility of an management committee.

Quality Lead Schools which can demonstrate and sustain very positive outcomes against each of the four key elements of the Achievement for All programme and lead other schools in the programme.

Quality Mark Schools which can demonstrate very positive outcomes against each of the four key elements of the programme after the initial two years can continue to participate in Achievement for All through the Quality Mark scheme.

Short-term plan A working document detailing daily teaching practice and all related aspects. It is informed by ongoing observational assessment and is often altered on a day-to-day basis.

Special school A school, with specialist staff and facilities, for pupils with SEND.

Strategic plan This is an expression of how an organisation intends to achieve its vision, mission, and aims in a deliverable form for a period beyond the current setting or financial year.

Teaching assistant (TA) Works alongside a classroom teacher to support the learning of pupils within a primary, secondary and/or special school.

Values The ideals that a person aspires to in his or her life which act as a point of reference to judgements and conduct, and according to which he or she conforms (or not) in relations with the social group of reference (community, society, culture).

Virtual school An approach, implemented and developed through the local authority, to oversee the educational attainment of LAC and, in some cases, those in post-16 provision. It acts as a single school with the aim of providing stability for LAC to raise their attainment and improve attendance. (Many local authorities have appointed a Virtual School Head (VSH) to oversee the education of LAC; the Children and Families Bill will make the appointment of a VSH statutory for all local authorities).

Vision An overall view of what the senior leadership team envisage for the school in the long term, i.e., where you would want it to be in ten years' time. The vision is usually expressed in a statement which would be reflected in the school's aims and organisational practice.

Vision statements These are precise goals which show where an organisation will be in the future. It moves an organisation forward from where it is now to where it would like to be.

Index